Table of Contents

Reading Vasily Grossman in the 21st century

Izak Dimenstein

Reading Vasily Grossman
in the 21st century

Izak B. Dimenstein

ISBN: 9798873189267

Acknowledgment

Thanks to Simon and Eugene Dimenstein for editorial and technical support in the publication of this book.

Preface

Vasily Grossman, a Soviet Russian writer of the mid-20th century, died in 1964. Among intellectuals in the West, his novel *Life and Fate* is now considered one of the remarkable fine literary works of the last century. The book was arrested by the KGB in 1961. It was published abroad in 1980 and eventually in the Soviet Union in 1989, two years before the country disappeared from the world map.

For many years, Grossman was almost forgotten. According to his primary English translator, Robert Chandler, Grossman's writing is now read in almost every European country. Multiple scholarly articles appeared in Russia but predominately abroad.

The Vasily Grossman Study Center in Turin, Italy, the world hub for Grossman scholars, organized World conferences (2006 and 2009) with two books of essays. St Peter's College, University of Oxford organized an *Interdisciplinary Symposium Vasily Grossman: Ruthless Truth in the Totalitarian Century* in 2011. International Scientific Conference *The Legacy of Vasily Grossman: Originality of the Classic of the XX Century* was organized by Turin's Study Center Vasily Grossman in Moscow in 2014.

Two comprehensive biographies were published: *The Life and Fate of Vasily Grossman* by John and Carol Garrard in the United Kingdom in 2012 and *Vasily Grossman and the Soviet Century* by Alexandra Popoff in the USA in 2019.

Three volumes of Grossman's biography *Vasiliĭ Grossman: literaturnaī̆a biografii ā v istoriko-politicheskom kontekst* [Vasily Grossman: literary biography in the historic-political context] were published in Russia by David Feldman, Yuriy Bit-Yunan in 2020. There is no translation into English.

This short book-length biographical essay differs from those already published biographies. It is written by a layperson in the literature research field that determines the presentation of the material. The book is designed in a workshop style with diagrams. This style adapts to a modern person's TV and now video clip way of consuming information.

Part One presents biographical data by concentrating on Grossman's last four years of life and the milieu around that time. Part Two focuses on his literary work after the Second World War with special attention to the book's publication ordeals. The Appendices include a hodgepodge collection of references and essay-like material that would not fit in the main biographical narrative but might add some nuance to it.

The current biography aims to draw attention to Vasily Grossman, a political philosopher by mindset and a writer in the tradition of Russian classic literature. The goal is to bring him into social discourse by reading, or for some, rereading in the 21st century. His books allude to the unlearned lessons of the previous century, which have become so visible during current events in the world, as a warning of the dangerous consequences if the rising aggressive authoritarianism could not be stopped.

The reluctant rebel
Introductory remarks

Grossman preached humanism even during the devastating conditions of the Second World War. Being a genuine product of the Soviet system, Grossman revealed its similarity to German Nazism. He rebelled in the form of fine literature with the *Stalingrad* and *Life and Fate* duology and other books, the sole tool in his possession.

In presenting Grossman's literary work, I traced his gradual transformation from a devoted participant of the Soviet Union Communist Party propaganda machine into an intellectual dissident.

I would call Grossman a reluctant rebel. Both words can be disputed as matters of opinion. While "reluctant" is more or less understandable as a person's desire to keep the comfortable, self-preserving cocoon intact, together with "rebel," it requires some clarification.

It is commonly accepted to define a dissident as a person who challenges an established political system or belief. In other words, a person who goes against the current is a dissident. One becomes a rebel in the implementation of dissent. Of course, this distinction is more complicated and nuanced and is explored in the literature. Apparent examples are the Dutch philosopher Baruch Spinoza and Russian writer Leo Tolstoy, who were ex-communicated from their religious denominations in the past. Modern-time dissidents existed in Eastern Europe and the Soviet Union.

Grossman as dissidents' herald in the Soviet Union

Can the definitions of a dissident or rebel be applied to Grossman, a well-established Soviet Russian writer? Grossman only wrote books and wanted to publish them under the conditions of that time. He did not give interviews then, as is habitual now. He did not write articles, except for a few perhaps ordered by authorities.

In Grossman's time, immediately after the Second World War, the term dissident was not used in the Soviet Union. It became habitual in the 1970s to refer to groups of intellectuals who challenged the Soviet regime regarding violating human rights.

When the KGB seized the manuscript of *Life and Fate* on February 14, 1961, there were no dissidents in the Soviet Union. Alexander Solzhenitsyn published the story *One Day in the Life of Ivan Denisovich* in 1962. *The Gulag Archipelago* was published abroad in 1967. Grossman's *Everything Flows...* was published abroad in 1970. *Life and Fate* was published abroad in Switzerland in 1980.

Grossman's rebel seeds grew when the conditions were ready. He might have considered himself no more than a benign dissident, but the regime accepted him as a traitor—a dangerous rebel. In reality, the Communist Party was right. He was a silenced and suppressed harbinger of the future dissident movement that contributed to the fall of the Communist Party's rule in Eastern Europe and the Soviet Union's dismissal.

Why the reluctant rebel?

After reading all of Grossman's published literary work, as well as perhaps most about him, I consider there to be a great deal of self-preservation in his personal and social life, although his behavior at war was marked by extraordinary courage. He had justified reasons to be cautious, especially bearing in mind that as a Jew, he wrote about Jewish issues at the time of the explosion of governmental antisemitism in the Soviet Union.

Grossman was a Soviet man, but his faith in the regime couldn't survive the many atrocities he witnessed growing in opposition to the heartless barbarities of the totalitarian state. Grossman's literary work after the Second World War is a reluctant denunciation of Socialism. Grossman's rebellion was in rejecting the devastating effects of both almost identical communist and fascist totalitarian regimes on people's lives.

There was no conformism in the form of self-preservation. Grossman's reluctance as a rebel consisted of understanding the need to preserve the fabric of people's existence, a person's dwelling. Grossman was close to the French philosophers Jean-Paul Sartre and Albert Camus, who were proponents of existentialism around the same time just after the Second World War. Grossman's rebellion was in a similar mold. (See *Camus's question in The Rebel essay* in the Appendices where in *Albert Camus and Vasily Grossman* article this subject is discussed in more detail.)

PART ONE

Vasily Grossman

Vasily Semyonovich Grossman

Yosif Solomonovich Grossman

Vasya

Vasily Grossman – the name for encyclopedia, search engines, etc.

Vasily Semyonovich –with a patronymic name for polite use in the Russian-speaking world.

Yosif Solomonovich Grossman – legal name in the passport, subpoenas, and other official documents.

Vasya – the diminutive name used by parents, relatives, close friends, and by himself in letters.

The sections in Part One of the book are not a substitution for Grossman's comprehensive biography, but rather orientation material. It is more of a reference section for his personal life. The goal is to present circumstances in Grossman's life that could influence his actions or inactions. The main focus is on highlighting the details that can help better explore the final steps of Grossman's life journey.

Grossman's reluctant rebel formation, which is the focus of the presented book, occurred during this time. In this regard, the narrative is limited by the last years of Grossman's life when his main books were written.

After bringing up Grossman's biography data in chronological order, I try to display his milieu and some circumstances of his personal life that played a role in his dwelling, such as the particularities of his family relationships along with the description of Grossman's milieu after the *Life and Fate* manuscript arrest time.

The" Lucky Grossman" section tries to show the bitter irony of these words. Even residency addresses reflect particularities of his private life which reverberated in his books.

Family

Based on documents, memoirs, or published letters, the family tree diagram presents Grossman's immediate family, which in some way is related directly or indirectly to his life.

Grossman was born on December 12, 1905, in Berdichev city in Ukraine, Russian Empire, according to official documents. The latter remark is mentioned because there is no mutual agreement about the birthplace among biographers.

Grossman Yosif Solomonovich
born 12/25/1905

Semyon Osipovich
(Solomon Iosifovich)
Grossman
Father (1870-1956)

Yekaterina Savelievna
(Malka Zayvelevna)
Vitis
Mother (1871-1941)

siblings
Maria,
Vladimir (William),
Arnold

David Sherentsis,
(arrested 1938)
Victor, Peter,
Natasha

siblings
Anna (aunt Anuyta) Sherentsis,
Maria (Malina) Savelievna Beniash,
Elizaveta (Liza) Savelievna Almaz

Nadezhda (Nadya) Almaz

Comments to this diagram will include only details that can clarify some events or situations in Grossman's life that will be mentioned in the narrative.

There is no data on how Grossman's mother and father got married. More than likely, it was a civilian act, habitual in Europe at that time. Nevertheless, the marriage must be documented otherwise the child would be qualified as a bastard.

More important for Grossman's life in his youth accessibility to education was the parents' social status before the revolution. Both Grossman's parents stemmed from a Jewish merchants' group. They were able to travel and live abroad. Most importantly, they could afford an education abroad.

The mother's line

Mother – Yekaterina Savelievna Malka Zayevelevna) Vitis (1871-1941).

Among mother's sisters, Anna Aunt Anuyta, who had been married to Dr. David Sherentsis, played a substantial role in Grossman's life in Berdichev. Dr. Sherentsis was also an entrepreneur before the October Revolution. Grossman lived with his mother in Dr. Sherentsis' home till 1920. Aunt Anuyta died in 1936. Dr. Sherentsis was arrested in 1938 and disappeared after the arrest.

Grossman's mother lived with her slightly retarded niece Natasha, Dr. Sherentsis's daughter, in Berdichev until they were transferred to the ghetto after the German invasion and eventually killed in September 1941.

Elizabeth's (Liza) daughter Nadezhda (Nadya) Moiseevna Almaz played a substantial role in Grossman's first steps as a writer. She was exiled from 1933 to 1936 in Astrakhan, then to Vorkuta-Pechersk GULAG. She returned to Moscow in November 1939. She will be mentioned in many places in this narrative. She was born in 1897 in Berdichev. Since 1925, she was the secretary of   Solomon Abramovich Lozovsky, an old Communist Party member, and the head of the Soviet Information Bureau Sovinformburo, the most significant information agency during the war. Lozovsky was executed in 1952, as a member of the Jewish Anti-Fascist Committee.

Victor, Dr. Sherentsis' son, he lived later in Moscow. He was married to Klara. This Grossman's first cousin kept a copy of the Life and Fate manuscript which was KGB confiscated in 1961.

The father's line

Father- Semyon Osipovich (Solomon Ysifovich) Grossman (1870-1956).

Grossman's name Yosif is evidence that his father's dad was not alive at the time of his birth according to Jewish tradition to name children in honor of dead close relatives.

Grossman's father became a Social Democrat in 1902. In 1903, when the party split into two factions, he joined the so-called Mensheviks. He had relationships with BUND, the Jewish branch of the Social Democratic Party. Since 1906 he completely withdrew from political activity. At one point he went to Novosibirsk (a big city in Siberia) before his connection with BUND and Mensheviks was uncovered.

One of the brothers Vladimir (William) left Russian in 1900th. He was married to Zhennya [Jenny]. His son, Oscar, visited Moscow in 1962; Grossman met him in the Inturist hotel.

Another father's brother, Arnold, also left for the USA but moved to Germany from the USA. Arnold and his daughter Paula fled to Moscow after fascist rule was established in Germany. Grossman's cousin Paula was arrested and never heard of again. The second Arnold's daughter stayed with her non-Jewish mother. Arnold died in 1940 on Moscow's outskirts from pneumonia.

Grossman's father was buried in Moscow at the Vagan'kovo cemetery in 1956.

Marriages

In Grossman's time in Russia, marriage was one of the perhaps solely cohesive materials after the revolution experimentation and devastating wartime. The intellectual circles, which were the Grossman environment, had some particularities different from the entire societyThey are discussed in many memoirs and reference materials though with questionable reliability. The description will be as short as possible, just to highlight milestones and some details extracted from documents that might be significant to reflect Grossman's immediate surroundings.

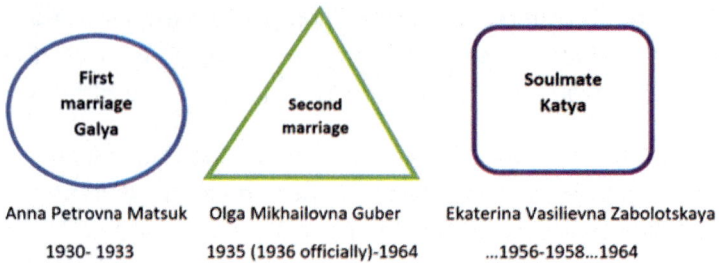

First marriage Galya	Second marriage	Soulmate Katya
Anna Petrovna Matsuk	Olga Mikhailovna Guber	Ekaterina Vasilievna Zabolotskaya
1930- 1933	1935 (1936 officially)-1964	...1956-1958...1964

First marriage Galya

During his studies at Moscow University, Grossman periodically visited Kiev where he met his old acquaintance, Galya. Excerpts from Grossman's letter to his father:

1928. ...: if it is the will of Allah, then apparently, I will marry, if not now, then in a year: I like my subject very much ("in love" I am embarrassed to write), I miss it mortally, I use full reciprocity, it seems that these conditions are necessary and sufficient for marriage. in February 1929: the insoluble problem of housing, as well as studying at universities in various cities, led to the fact that the husband spent most of the time in Moscow, and the wife - in Kiev.

Grossman got married in 1930. The same year his daughter, Katya, was born. Most of the time Katya spent with Grossman's mother in Berdichev.

From a letter to the father in August 1932:" *I decided to break up with Galya. Galya is not my wife. I don't like her, everything has burned down, there can be no situation in which we will live as before.*" Divorced in 1933. Galya's unfaithfulness is not supported by Grossman's statements but is presented in some of his father's letters. This issue remains at the level of rumors.

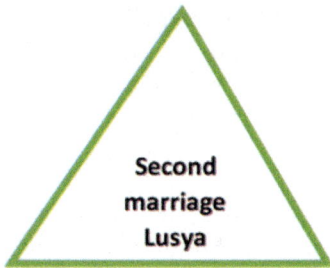

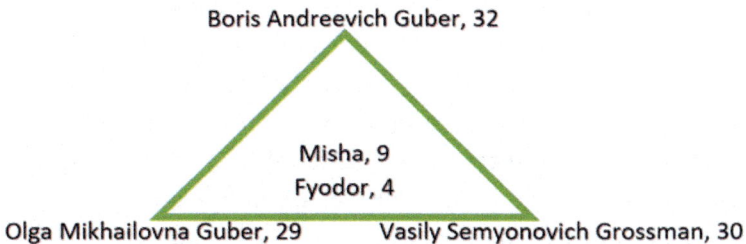

**Second
marriage
Lusya**

Boris Andreevich Guber, 32

Misha, 9
Fyodor, 4

Olga Mikhailovna Guber, 29   Vasily Semyonovich Grossman, 30

The classic love triangle is Boris Andreevich Guber, friend, and writer of a group "Pereval", his wife, Olga Mikhailovna Guber, and Vasily Semyonovich Grossman. The couple had two boys, Misha and Fyodor. Grossman and Olga Guber got married in 1936. Boris Guber was arrested and killed in 1937. Olga was arrested in 1938 and released after … month in prison. The story of Grossman's efforts to take his wife from prison is described in many versions. Micha was killed by an accident explosion of a mine in 1942 in Chistopol, where Grossman's family was evacuated. Grossman remained married to Olga till his death in 1964.

Soulmate
Katya

Grossman's involvement with Ekaterina Vasilievna Zabolotskaya, the wife of his friend and neighbor famous Russian poet Nikolay Alekseyevich Zabolotsky is for outsiders of this life drama a fascinating story, but for participants of this love square the ground for suffering. It is still waiting by itself for a dramatic fictional display or many of them, although it has a remote allusion to the *Life and Fate* novel.

Nikolay Alekseyevich Zabolotsky, 53 Vasily Semyonovich Grossman, 51

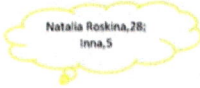

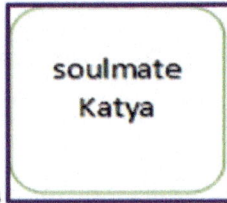

Natalia Roskina,28; Inna,5

soulmate
Katya

Nikita 23; Natasha 18 Fyodor Gruber24

Ekaterina Vasilievna Zabolotskaya,50   Olga Mikhailovna Gruber, 55

The dry chronology of the four angel love story follows such a sequence of events: being a family friend and neighbor in the writer's compound Begovaya, eventually, Grossman and Zabolotskaya get attracted to each other, falling in love resulting in Zabolotskaya and Grossman leaving their spouses in 1956 and settled in the room of a communal flat.

In the summer of 1958, both returned to their spouses. During this period, Nikolay Zabolotsky was involved with a woman Natalia Roskina. Zabolotskaya and Grossman remained steadfast to the end of Grossman's life. The entire story produced and revealed a beautiful Russian woman Ekaterina Zabolotskaya whose life story is waiting for a Shakespeare dramatist. Her photos can give a clue of how beautiful she was by the internal shine of her eyes. I am resisting the temptation to elaborate on this story, although inevitably, I will touch some sides of it later. According to commonly accepted views of some memoirists, his second wife, Olga Mikhailovna, had a tough character, while Ekaterina Vasilievna was the exact opposite: kind, soft, and friendly.

Daughter

Ekaterina Vasilievna Korotkova-Grossman (1930-2020).

The relationship with her father was complicated. After Grossman's mother's death, she lived with her mother Anna Matsuk, and her stepfather. Only for a short time, she lived with Grossman and Ekaterina Zabolotskaya in their single room on the Lomonosov Prospect in 1957.

At crucial moments, Grossman participated in his daughter's life. For example, after the car accident in Kharkiv. More than likely, he participated in her employment in Moscow.

She moved to Moscow after graduating from the Kharkiv Foreign Language College, English Department in 1955. She was employed by the Foreign Literature Library. She was a professional translator of English literature and a member of the Soviet Writers Union.

I would like to draw attention to her partonomic name-Vasilievna. According to rules in the former USSR, when a person reaches 16, the government issues a passport with lines of, last name, first name, partonomic name, if any, date and place of birth, and the nationality, the famous 5 point. The nationality could be chosen from the father or mother nationality. The patronymic name should follow from the birth certificate, where the father's name was Yosif. For practical reasons, of course, it would be better to have Grossman's pen name. More than likely, Grossman facilitated this legal procedure in 1946. In the former Soviet Union, being Vasilievna was better than Yosifovna.

In the 90th and later, she wrote some memory articles and gave interviews about her father, however, one of Grossman's letters from Armenia to Lipkin might characterize the relationships as crucial for him time in 1961, just after Life and Fate arrest catastrophe: "I received a congratulation and a letter from my daughter Katya. What a cold, indifferent letter, with what indifference it is written. And yet it's better what she wrote, and yet it's easier than her silence for 5 months."

Stepson

Fyodor Borisovich Guber (1931-2020). Grossman had not legally adopted Fyodor to maintain the memory of Fyodor's father, Boris Guber killed in 1937. Until Grossman died in 1964, they lived in the same apartment even after Fyodor got married to Irina Novikova in 1956 and her daughter Lena was born in 1958. After his mother died in 1988, Fyodor was with Grossman's daughter, Ekaterina Vasilievna Korotkova-Grossman, holder of all copyright on Grossman's publications. Fyodor had in possession the Grossman archive left in the apartment. In the 1990th, he published some Gerrards described him unfavorably regarding his role in Grossman's life. Irina Ehrenburg could not get support from ecovering the text of "The Hell of Treblinka" from archives.

Fyodor Grossman's second stepson, Misha, who old during evacuation in Chistopol in 1942, n by the patronymic name as a sign of not a father in Russian culture.

Biography Periods

☐

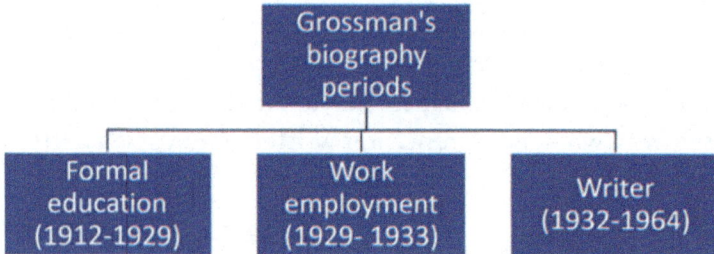

Formal education

The diagram below presets steps in Grossman's formal education. The educational facilities have specific names which are not used today. The periods are approximately adjusted to the steps in modern education to make it more understandable for a contemporary reader.

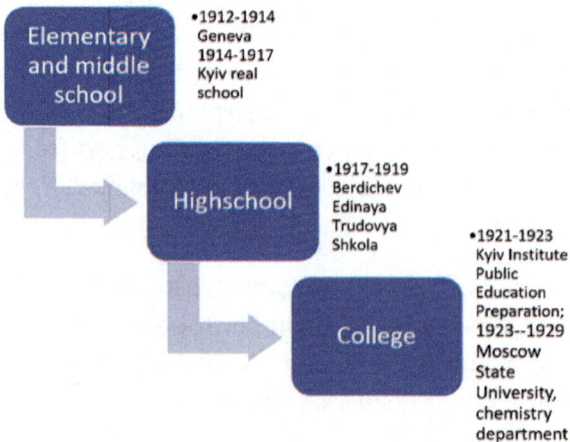

Employment work experience

The work experience diagram includes only employment besides Grossman's work as a professional writer which can be loosely defined as the beginning of 1930th.

Grossman worked on expeditions in Central Asia while being a student at Moskow University in 1928.

During his study as a chemical engineer at the university, Grossman practiced at a soap factory in 1929.

After graduating from the university, Grossman was employed in the Smolyanka-11 mine' laboratory in Makiivka from 1929-1930. Then he worked at the Institute of Pathology and Occupational Hygiene in Stalino during 1930-1932.

His work in the coal mine industry, as well as his employment at the Sacco & Vanzetti pencil factory in Moskow after returning from Donbas gave Grossman knowledge and experience for his literary work before the Second World War.

The mentioned in some source Grossman's work in a lumber factory is not documented and might be fake just to bring him into a worker category for eligibility for government education immediately after high school.

Main periods in Grossman's biography as a writer

The diagram below presents three periods of Grossman's work as a writer. They are defined as pre-war fiction, war journalism, and post-war fiction. During every period, especially during the war, there was a mixture of fiction and war correspondence with prevailing the latter. Grossman worked as a correspondent for the main military newspaper "Krasnaya Zvezda" (Red Star) from 1941 - 1945.

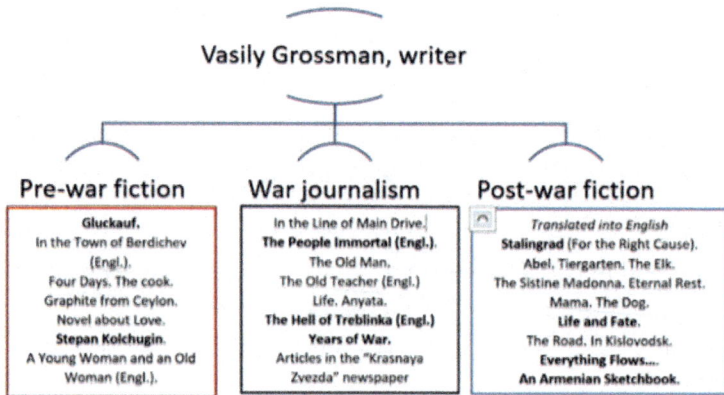

Vasily Grossman, writer

Pre-war fiction	War journalism	Post-war fiction
Gluckauf. In the Town of Berdichev (Engl.). Four Days. The cook. Graphite from Ceylon. Novel about Love. **Stepan Kolchugin.** A Young Woman and an Old Woman (Engl.).	In the Line of Main Drive. **The People Immortal (Engl.).** The Old Man. The Old Teacher (Engl.) Life. Anyata. **The Hell of Treblinka (Engl.)** **Years of War.** Articles in the "Krasnaya Zvezda" newspaper	*Translated into English* **Stalingrad** (For the Right Cause). Abel. Tiergarten. The Elk. The Sistine Madonna. Eternal Rest. Mama. The Dog. **Life and Fate.** The Road. In Kislovodsk. **Everything Flows....** **An Armenian Sketchbook.**

The diagram is not intended to be a registry of Grossman's literary work but rather the most significant list that reflects every period. The titles are placed in chronological sequence to reflect Grossman's evolution as a writer and a person. Some stories were updated by Grossman, but they are placed in the diagram at the time of the original publication. The publications translated into English are marked as (Engl.). Books are listed in bold.

Moskow residency addresses

Some introductory remarks

First of all, this section might have only a special interest for few readers and definitely can be omitted, but the addresses play a role in understanding of residency in Grossman's life.

Grossman's dwelling addresses have a certain interest because this place had had definite influence on this writing and personal life for worse and for good. Not understandable for a reader in the West, but perhaps even for a reader in Russia now, the question of life dwelling was one of the most contentious during Grossman's lifetime.

In *Master and Margarita* novel, M.A. Bulgakov ironically put in Satan's words about people *"The apartment question only spoiled them ..."* Without going into the multiple interpretations of this phrase, the living place in Moscow was a real problem due to many reasons.

The addresses presented in these materials are predominately extracted from Grossman's letters exchanges with the sender's return address, as the more reliable source. The correct addresses are significant in following the sequence of events, because there were simultaneous different flat occupations.

Writers became the privileged class only in the late 1930th with special apartments, modest by West standards, but highly valuable under Moscow's shortness of "real estate" conditions. While taming writers as part of the propaganda machine, the government presented Litfond dachas, attachments to special hospitals, closed food distributors, and canteens. But this occurred much later than Grossman started to live and work in literature. At that time, every square foot in a communal apartment was a treasure.

From Grossman's letters to his father in October 1928: "I was sickened by the lack of my corner. This need to travel from acquaintances to acquaintances is very nerve-wracking, and sometimes steps on self-respect. Hired a room – the room is unimportant, small, out of town, 30 r. per month; better than last year's in the sense that you don't have to travel by train (only by tram) and that it's warm".

1930- 1933- in the Nadya Almaz apartment until her arrest.

1935- 1938 – in Olga Gruber's sister Eugenia's apartment.

1938 -1947 - Herzen street 14/2 app. 108, in the center of Moscow downtown. As a member of the Soviet Writers Union since 1937, Grossman received two rooms in a communal apartment sharing this flat with two families.

Since 1947 the main Grossman's address was Begovaya Street (Беговая) 1A building 3, apartment 1.

This flat Grossman occupied with his wife Olga Mikhailovna Gruber, her son Fyodor, and the house helper Natalia Ivanovna Darenskya. When Fyodor got married in 1956, his wife Irina Novikova lived there. Their daughter Lena was born in 1958.

In 1954, Grossman received a room in a communal apartment like a working study on Lomonosovsky Avenue, 15, building 10c, app. 9. He lived there with Ekaterina Vasilievna Zabolotskaya from 1956- Spring of 1958.

The last Grossman's address that appeared on one of his letters on February 4th, 1963, is Moscow, Second Aeroport street 16/252 (2-я Аэропортовская) in one of three 9-store buildings of Writers Union cooperative erected near the Aeroport Metro station at the end of 1961. Grossman lived there for a short time. In the same building's section but in apartment 241 lived Ekaterina Vasilievna Zabolotskaya. Now the address is Begovaya Street 23 as part of the Third Transport Circle (Трétьe трáнспортное кольцó, ТТК) around the Moscow. The changes in the number of addresses of the same buildings might bring some confusion.

From Boris Yampolsky's sketch, "The Last Meeting with Vasily Grossman": On an incomplete square hectare lived almost five hundred poets, novelists, satirists, writers of operetta librettos, sketches, completists, modern meistersingers... It was a nine-story cooperative house...In one of these cells, in a modest and cramped box of a one-room apartment with windows into a quiet deserted parallelogram of the courtyard, also moved Vasily Semyonovich Grossman.

The presented Grossman's addresses can serve as reference data, but it would be interesting to draw attention to the Russian culture location of the mid-20th century that can be loosely defined as Begovaya 1a.

Russia's cultural landmark

Immediately after WWII at the end of 1947, the western outskirts of Moscow just where the Khoroshovskoye chosse merged with Begovaya Street were constructed four flat brick two-story buildings. They had a common address Begovaya 1a. The complex belonged to the Moscow Writer Association, a type of cooperative, but there was another representative of Moscow's cultural elite.

For these materials, the narrative is exceptionally important that at this place generated masterpieces of Russian literature of the second half of the XX century. Zabolotsky, one of the first cohort of Russian poets, wrote his "Late Love" cycle of poems.

Grossman wrote his Life and Fate novel there. This was the place of Grossman's manuscript confiscation by the KGB.

Begovaya Street was Grossman's Yasnaya Polyana, the former estate of Leo Tolstoy. In contrast to Tolstoy's mansion, which is even now a landmark of world literature, Grossman created his main book in an apartment on the first floor of one of four flat buildings. Behind the buildings was an empty field. Nearby, within walking distance, was Vagan'kovo cemetery.

By coincidence, WWII German prisoners participated in the construction of these "buildings", maybe some of them participated in the Stalingrad battle in 1942.

The most significant is that Grossman's close friend, the famous Russian poet and translator Semyon Lipkin (build 8 app. 10).

The Grossman Memory Plague was placed on the 2nd Airport 23 (now Kranoarmeyskya Street, 25) building in 2009.

☐

"Lucky Grossman"

"Lucky Grossman" (coined by writer Ilya Ehrenburg) was a continuing legend during the war as a correspondent when he had managed to go through most bloodies events from the Stalingrad battle to the Berlin operation without even being wounded. He crossed the Volga River in Stalingrad under the fire. It was an episode when a grenade just had not exploded nearby. He had a reputation for personal bravery.

However, Grossman's life, ironically including as a writer, was permeated with fear of real dangers. Even an arrest could be on the table, perhaps except for a short war period. He had definite reasons for it during Stalin's time with different levels of certainty. Fear was in the skin of all people in the USSR Jews particularly. Years of terror contributed to this feeling of personal vulnerability. Society in general accepted this vulnerability as a kind of norm. Grossman, like other Soviet citizens gradually became used to the permanent fear atmosphere.

When my aunt Hannha Rosenthal, a Communist Party functionary, who had been arrested many times in bourgeois pre-Soviet Latvia, was arrested for not being cautious about talking in a close circle of her peers, she was blamed by relatives for recklessness rather than expressing the authority's condemnation for taking away a mother of 5 years old daughter in the Siberia Gulag.

The diagram presents the apparent source which could be for Grossman as danger an arrest.

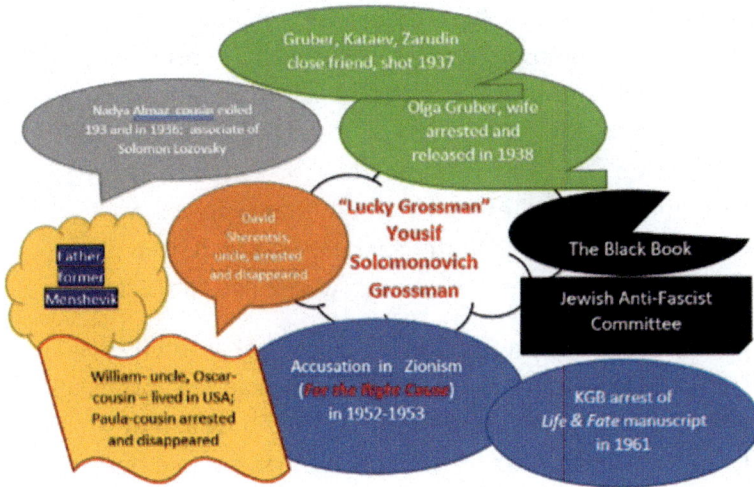

Grossman's father (Semyon Osipovich) was an RSDRP member since 1903. He joined the Menshevik fraction in 1905. He kept a low profile after the revolution because it was not completely safe to have a Menshevik story. Lenin sent Martov, the head of the Menshevik fraction, into exile in 1920. The authorities did not appreciate the presence of relatives abroad. Grossman had known him and probably unknown relatives abroad from both sides. The father's brother William lived in the USA. When his son Oscar visited Moscow and Grossman met him, this was noticed by the KGB. Grossman mentioned an aunt from his mother's side in an official review questionnaire.

In 1933, he witnessed the search in the Nadezhda Moiseevna Almaz, his cousin after her arrest where he lived at that time. He was also of interest during the search.

His papers also (the manuscript of, the novel Gluckauf, were seized. Nadya Almaz, his cousin, well connected, the secretary of Solomon Lozovsky (the head of Profintern, member of Comintern, Head of Soviet Information Bureau [Sovinformburo] during the war, Head of Jewish Anti-Fascist Committee [JAC]), was arrested as Trotskyite in 1933. Grossman lived in her apartment at that time. He was interrogated because in the apartment search his name appeared as Grossman IS. Nadya was exiled to Astrakhan.

Grossman was connected with the Pereval group (Boris Guber, Ivan Kataev, Nikolay Zarudin, Alexander Voronsky). Boris Guber was his close friend and the husband of Grossman's wife Olga till 1935. Grossman's name began appearing in the informer's reports. In 1937, they were arrested allegedly for a plot to kill the NKVD chief Ezow. Grossman was subpoenaed for questions. Grossman visited among other luminaries Ezow's wife Evgenia Chayutina.

Grossman's wife Olga was arrested in 1938. It is well well-known story of how Grossman was interrogated, and fought for Olga's release after three months, including his letters to high-level authorities, including to Yezhov.

The exiled cousin (Nadya Almaz) and the executed friends (the Pereval group) could be serious kompromat material.

 Grossman and his mother lived in his mother's sister's Anna (Aunt Anyuta) home for many years. The house belonged to Dr. David Sherentsis, Anna's husband. Dr. Sherentsis was arrested and disappeared in 1938. The reason for the uncle's arrest was not known but during the 1937 mass arrest authorities had just a plan for the number of arrests.

Grossman's friendship with Leonid Taratura, the son executed in 1937 by Alexander Taratuta, also could be unfavorable under certain conditions.

Grossman's participation in The Black Book was not safe after the antisemitic companies, especially after the Jewish Anti-Fascist Committee (JAC) arrest and execution. Grossman was a member of JAC, but it was a loose organization with many participants and friendly connections with the most prominent member of the executive committee. It was a black mark. Who could predict the behavior of a tortured victim? Lev Sheinin, senior investigator of the USSR Prosecutor's Office for especially important cases, was arrested - in October 1951 and confessed to belonging to a group of nationalist writers. In the circle of his like-minded people, Sheinin included Ehrenburg and Grossman.

Accusation in Zionism was the main theme during the discussion of the For the Right Cause in January 1953 just when the "Doctors Plot" was brewing. Grossman found out about Stalin's death on March 5th, 1953, while "hiding" at his friend Semyon Lipkin's dacha in Iliencovo, outside Moscow.

"Lucky Grossman" was reserved for an internal purpose as only capable of creating a War and Peace-like monumental literature work to immortalize Stalin's achievement. Grossman became a big fish in a small pound of writers in the Soviet Union, especially after talented writers were exiled and purged by Stalin who personally overlooked the writer's business. The Writers Union bosses perhaps knew where the winds blew from, but Grossman might not be aware of this.

After Stalin's death, the short window was not open enough to tolerate the continuation of the duology. In essence, the regime only cut off some excesses but was the same totalitarian nature. Grossman, however, had changed. He produced an unprintable variant of Life and Fate at that time. He worked on Everything Flows meanwhile from 1955 till his death.

Grossman, like millions of Soviet citizens, was accustomed to an atmosphere of constant fear. Grossman had a personal reason of fear in refusing to sign the letter. The likelihood of arrest would increase. The antisemitic background was apparent in the For a Just Cause book critical campaign. The presence of relatives abroad, and contacts with them could be the ground for accusations at that time. Grossman refused to communicate with his friend's relative (Natalia Roskina) who came from the USA.

We know about the action that was exerted on Grossman. Perhaps some of them are unknown to us. Grossman suspected the close monitoring of him by the KGB. His behavior can be understood. The KGB archive opened for a short time in 1991 revealed that the KGB Chief Vladimir Semychastny reported to the Central Committee of the Communist Party about conversations in Grossman's home after the Life and Fate manuscript arrest. The source of the information remains unknown.

According to the Fyodor Guber's memoir: "Apparently, our apartment was being monitored. In this regard, it should be said that shortly before the arrest of the Life and Fate novel, a neighbor who lived above us received a call at the door from young people with suitcases and relevant documents in the afternoon. They asked her to stay out of the apartment for a while. On this day, my mother heard a knock upstairs over the room in which Grossman's office was.

Grossman didn't feel safe in his home. Neither his stepson Fyodor Guber, nor his wife Olga Mikhailovna Guber were supportive, to say softly, when he wrote Everything Frows... Even in the hospital during his last days, according to Anna Berser, Grossman used jests to discuss his Everything Flows suspecting KGB agents among the personnel and overhearing devices in his ward.

Excerpt from Boris Yampolsky sketch "The last meeting with Vasily Grossman" when he entered Grossman's apartment on (November 15, 1963: " he [Grossman] put his finger to his lips, and silently led me ... into ... room, where on a table ...was a sheet of paper ... was written: "Borya, keep in mind, the walls may have ears." A construction technician told one of the board members that the apartment was "voiced"

WWII time ironically was for Grossman the safest period of life despite all the real dangers of being wounded and killed by real fire. He became one of the most popular writers in the country.

☐

Life and Fate manuscript arrest

The diagram below presents three periods of Grossman's life before the Life and Fate manuscript's arrest (February, 14th 1961) in the following characteristics: troubling thunder after the publication of the If You Believe the Pythagoreans play, the dangerous storm during the publication ordeal of the Stalingrad (For a Just Cause) novel, and the publication outcome Life and Fate manuscript, which final destiny remained unknown for Grossman until his death.

The play *If You Believe the Pythagoreans* was written before the war but published in Znamya magazine in 1946. The publication coincided with notorious Communist Party materials for the postwar repression of intellectual life in the Soviet Union. Grossman had gotten some critical articles, including in the central newspaper Pravda. This was thunder before the real storms during and after the Stalingrad/For a Just Cause publication ordeal. During the late 1950s through the beginning of 1953, Grossman was in real trouble at the level of even expecting an arrest, that culminated at the time of the "Doctor's Plot". In 1959 Grossman finished the second part of the duology Life and Fate novel. He brought his manuscript to the Znamya magazine in October 1960.

The magazine signed a contract with Grossman and even paid him appropriate money as an advance sum, the publication was on the holt.

The novel was unpublishable. Instead of returning the manuscript to the author, the novel was forwarded to the Communist Party Central Committee propaganda department, which decided to confiscate all copies of the manuscript.

Znamya published many of Grossman's works before, especially during the war. As a former military correspondent, Grossman made a combat reconnaissance what in Russian sound razvedka boem. This military action assumes casualties. "The Lucky Grossman" was wounded falling in an ambush, but he fought even wounded.

The common belief is that Grossman was naïve and behaved fullish giving the manuscript to Znamya magazine. Perhaps, naïve in maintaining hopes, but completely rational and smart. The diagram presents how smartly Grossman distributed his ammunition.

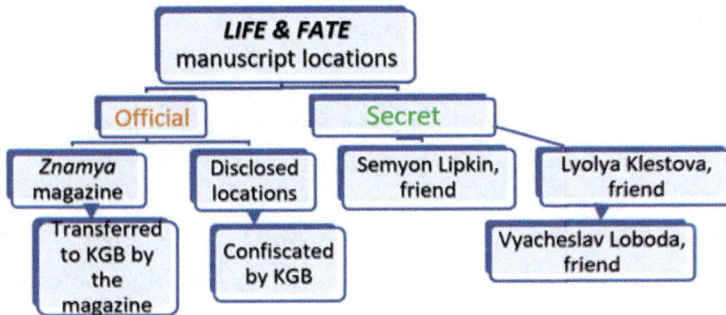

Lyola Klestova is like Lyola Dominikina, a friend from his student day at Moscow University. Before Grossman died, he had transferred the manuscript from Lyola to Vyacheslav Loboda in Maloyaroslavets 150 km (93 ml) from Moscow. In late 1988, Vyacheslav's widow returned the manuscript to Fyodor Guber, Grossman's stepson.

The diagram below demonstrated how Grossman outwitted KGB agents pretending to comply with their demands. They took the manuscript even from Grossman's cousin, Victor, apartment.

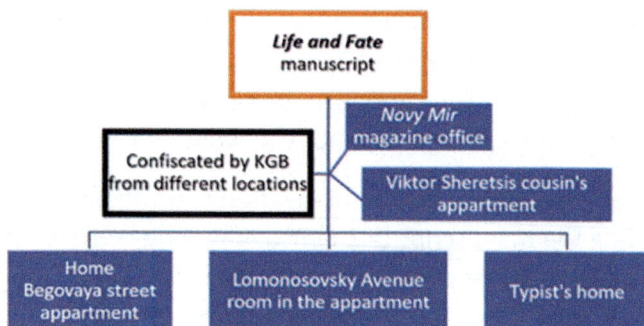

Grossman continued to fight for the return of his manuscript. He had even met with the "grey cardinal" the Communist Party ideology High Priest M.A. Suslov.

In her memoir *Farewell*, Anna Berser mentions Grossman's words about the novel short before his death: "I'd like to hold it in my hands... In a few minutes: - I'd like to reread it..." An excerpt from Grossman's letter to Lipkin about the finished Life and Fate novel on October 24, 1959: "Am I right? That's the first thing, the main thing. Am I right before people, and therefore- right before God?

Milieu after *Life and Fate* manuscript arrest

The time after the Life and Fate manuscript confiscation by the KGB could be substantial for Grossman 's consolidation of his views. Everything Flows… started in parallel with Life and Fate and left unfinished was the place where Grossman could say things that he considered unprintable in that social environment. In An Armenian Sketchbook, Grossman combined both in a printable in his view form of a traveler chat.

It would not be a great revelation if we state that a person's life from a celebrity to a modest farmer also occurs in a different-sized micro tribe environment. Grossman's immediate surroundings might determine his last work and state of mind. An approximate diagram with comments can give some knowledge of Grossman's surroundings in the 1960s.

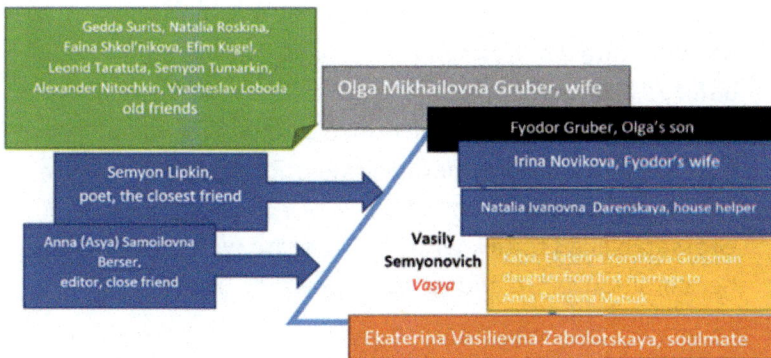

All of the diagram's "participants" were or will be mentioned in different places of these materials. The mentioned friends are calling Grossman respectfully in Russian culture the patronymic name Semyonovich or diminutive home name Vasya.

The diagram is designed in such a form that family members are placed to the right, but friends are to the left. The friends' names are extracted from Grossman's letters to his friend Semyon Lipkin published by Lipkin's wife Inna Lisnyanskaya's daughter Elena Makarova. This set of letters is more reliable than letters published by Lipkin in his memoirs about Grossman. Lipkin selected them and sometimes "edited" for publication. The same did Fyodor Guber in his memoir.

Olga Mikhailovna, Grossman's wife, his daughter Katya, the stepson Fyodor, and Ekaterina Vasilievna Zabolotskaya already were mentioned in the Family section. The Grossman family issues are presented in Gerrard with many details, including some interviews in the 1990s. Nevertheless, some comments might be appropriate.

Natalia (Natasha) Ivanovna Darenskya was Fyodor's nanny before his father, Boris Gruber, was arrested in 1937. She lived with Grossman's family since 1945 as a home helper. According to Fyodor's memoir, she once said to Grossman: "Although you're a Jew, but a saint." As Fyodor remarked, Grossman liked to talk with this illiterate woman cherishing her common sense and wisdom. She died in 1964.

A letter to Lipkin on January 11th, 1962, after Grossman left Armenia might reflect the complicated relationships in the family affairs: "I received a very heavy letter from Begovya from O.M. [Olga Mikhailovna, his wife]. I wrote to her that I knew that Katya [Zabolotskaya] was going to Sochi, but that confusion."

Irina Novikova was at home when the Life and Fate manuscript was confiscated by the KGB on February 14th, 1961. Her father spent many years in Gulag. Grossman had with him interesting conversations.

During the 1960s, the last period of Grossman's life, he severed his connections with the literary community, especially after the "novel's withdrawal", as it was officially defined the Life and Fate manuscript forcible seizure by KGB. For many of Grossman's friends, he was toxic, if we use modern terms, at least undesirable for communication, but Grossman from his side hasn't had any desire for contacts.

Grossman's personal life was complicated by an unhappy to the end marriage with Olga Guber, a happy but controversial relationship with his soulmate Ekaterina Zabolotskaya, a cool relationship with his daughter Katya, and perhaps hostile, at least cool, with Olga's son Fyodor Guber.

Lipkin Semyon Izrailevich, the closest friend since 1950th, poet and translator, and author of memoirs of Grossman. He will be often mentioned in these materials, including excerpts from his memoirs and Grossman's letters to him. His memoirs are the main source of knowledge about Grossman's personal life.

Berser Anna (Asya) Samoilovna (1917–1994), one of the editors of the Novy Mir's magazine (1958–1971). She wrote the passionate memoir book about Grossman and his last days titled "The Farewell" published in 1990 together with Lipkin's memoir.

Besides Lipkin and Berser, below is the list of writers with whom Grossman communicated in the 1960s, probably incomplete but extracted from Grossman's letter to Lipkin.

 Pismenny Alexander (1909—1971); Gecht Symon writer (1903–1963), close friend; Munblit Georgy (1904–1994), writer; he participated in The Black Book together with Grossman; Fayerman Ruvim, writer, (1891–1972); Pen'kovsky, translator, (1894–1971), friend of Grossman and Lipkin; Moran Ruvim, writer (1908–1986); Yamposky Boris, writer, (1912–1972), Ehrenburg Irene writer (1911–1997), Yilia Ehrenburg's daughter; Tumarkin Semyon, mathematician, youth friend.

Vyacheslav Ivanovich Loboda, a friend of Grossman, his wife Vera, and children - Maria and Lyudmila. The friendship arose when Loboda and Grossman rented a couple of rooms in Kozitsky Lane in Moskow during their student time.

According to Vyacheslav's wife, returning from Grossman's funeral, he laid on a couch the entire day turning his face to the wall. Vyacheslav died in a car accident.

 Loboda's family kept a complete copy of Grossman's novel Life and Fate in Maloyaroslavets.

In Armenia

Grossman lived less the four years after the novel's confiscation. In the fall of 1961, he left for Armenia to translate a book by an Armenian author using an interlinear. The details of this arrangement would be out of place in this mostly biographical section, especially if there are some conflicting materials in this regard.

For Grossman, two and a half months out of Moscow were a kind of respite. He enjoyed Armenia, his travels, and meeting different people unrelated to the writer community. And a new book was percolation through his mind that finalized in An Armenian Sketchbook.

In this part of the section, it would be reasonable to concentrate on the state of Grossman's physical shape that inevitably influenced everything that he did. Unfortunately, the sources are scarce, limited to fragments of Grossman's letters to Lipkin's memoir.

From some letters to Lipkin, it appears that he was not well in Armenia.

November 9th, 1961: I'm not very healthy here, but now it seems to be better. Perhaps, some acclimatization. But later he wrote periodically in this way.

December 2nd, 1961: I was so tired that apart from a nervous breakdown and a senseless desire to cry – I didn't feel anything – I completely blurted out.

December 11th, 1961: From fatigue, my working capacity decreased, and I got tired quickly... in the evenings his face and forehead were covered with purple spots.

Grossman refers to his age as advanced in modern terms. For example, some remarks: Well, what, it's an episode in my life, and even at the end of my life, the life lived; ... the elderly gentleman works on his [the author] book. Grossman's book on Armenia originally was titled Traveler's Notes of an Advanced Years Person —

There are traces of Grossman's deteriorating health even in An Armenian Sketchbook, although some descriptions of his physical problems should not be literary, because they are a part of the plot in the book.

However, interesting and remarkable is Grossman's letter to his soul mate Ekaterina Zabolotskaya while in Armenia on November 29th, 1961: "You made me laugh and frightened me with wishing me to be a sheep. It's bad for lambs in Armenia — so many of them are cut here! I've seen so many bloody sheep name for a donkey] - he is not eaten, but only beaten, moreover, he is stubborn and can pull hard uphill - all this is necessary for a Russian writer."

The letter reflects Grossman's high spirit at that time. He was ready for *An Armenian Sketchbook*, his farewell poem in prose.

Last period of life

We do not have reliable data about Grossman's disease that ended his life. A few remarks can be found in Lipkin's memoir that are repeated by biographers sometimes with confusing errors. Garrards even called the disease stomach cancer. The disease had influenced all his decisions and behavior.

The diagram reflects the sequence of events that we know so far. The diagram will be followed with an excerpt from Lipkin's memoir and some of my comments.

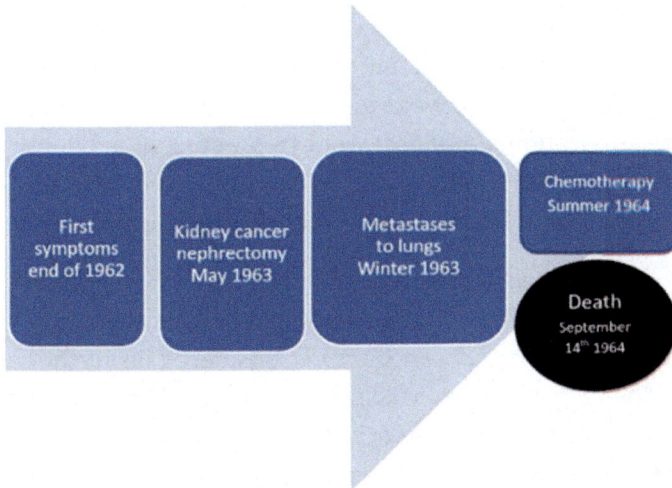

First symptoms end of 1962 → Kidney cancer nephrectomy May 1963 → Metastases to lungs Winter 1963 → Chemotherapy Summer 1964 → Death September 14th 1964

According to Lipkin's memoir, Grossman noticed blood in urine at the end of 1962. The Writers Union clinic internal medicine doctor recommended seeing a urologist.
Both Grossman and Lipkin thought that blood in urine might be connected with spicy food consumed during the trip to Armenia almost a year ago. But he sometimes complained about his health, which was unusual for him before.

In April 1963, the bad symptoms recurred. Grossman was arranged in Botkin Hospital in May where the nephrectomy was performed. The surgeon was not sure that there were any metastases. Excerpt from Ekaterina Zabolotskaya's letter to Semyon Lipkin on May 11, 1963: "... Bedsores in poor condition - wet. There was a pustule on his chest again, and the day before, yesterday, a pustule broke through in the nose.... he has become even sadder, more depressed." Bedsores are evidence of poor nursing and care. Pustules represent a disseminated infectious process.

Grossman was told about nephritis or a cyst, according to different sources. However, according to the above-cited letter: "Today, when he went to the window for the first time after the operation, he said: "I went to breathe air and look through the windows of the cancer institute." The Botkin Hospital was adjacent to Herzen Oncology Research Institute.

At the beginning of Winter 1963, Grossman was hospitalized in the Botkin Hospital. According to Lipkin: Grossman was diagnosed with lung cancer. Doctors considered his further stay in the hospital meaningless. One of them said, "Let him die at home." In the final months from June 1964 till his death in September 1964, Grossman had spent in a hospital for so-called chemotherapy. It was an in modern terms hospice store wooden house in a regular community hospital.

The last days

Grossman's final days are described by his friend Anna Berser in her memoir book "Farewell" published in 1990. She participated in taking companionship at Grossman's bedside in turns with other members of family and friends. Some excerpts from this book would be appropriate to present in this section by avoiding the temptation to place almost the entire book. However, more excerpts will be placed in the Appendices in the material about memoirs on Grossman.

Anna Berser's notes show the man who courageously carried his fate of a dying fighter for life. Suspected to be bugged by the KGB in the hospital, he communicated often with gestures. Below are some of the notes from the book in italics.

"It was not a nervously torn soul, but even on the verge of death, harmoniously natural and alive. All the countless catastrophes with his clean books have not distorted his personality. They brought him death, but life on its moral heights did not distort it. There was not a shadow of a dark focus on himself alone."

"Two days before his death, on Friday, when I wrote about him at home on a piece of paper: "Bad, very bad, terrible," he met me with the words: "Tell me what new things happened? With this question — in different ways, in different forms, and different words — he always met me."

"After his death, I was asked very often: did not even a person like Grossman understand what he was sick with, did not understand that he was dying? And how was it to explain, without coarsening his image, that he understood everything, knew everything, and called it in his own words? How many times did he repeat the lines: It's hard to die: It's good to die, written by the dying Nekrasov [Nikolay Alexandrovich Nekrosov, famous Russian XIX century poet]. But a person of such powerful connections with life cannot live without hope for life."

"And with the watch was also hard. He didn't take it off his hand. He looked very often, and when it got worse and he could not find a place for himself, he endlessly raised his hand and peered into the dial. It was so tragic that I didn't have the strength to look at it. He seemed to be looking at the clock to see how long he had left to live.

Only on the day of his death did he remove the watch from his hand. And clearly and sharply separated himself from life. It was the only day he didn't ask what was new in life, what was heard in the Novy Mir magazine. It was the only day he showed no interest in the printed items. That was the only day he didn't ask to sit next to him. And when I arrived, I heard a clear, even distinct voice of his: Darling, go home. Why would you suffer...

Grossman died on September 14, 1964. Grossman's mother was massacred in Berdichev on September 15, 1941.

Grossman wrote two letters to his slayed mother on September 15, 1950, and on September 14, 1961.

The grave

In his published 1984 memoir about Grossman, S.I. Lipkin, wrote: "Grossman's relatives, E. V. Zabolotskaya and I wanted to bury an urn with ashes in the Vagan'kovo cemetery, next to the grave of Grossman's father, close to Begovaya, where Grossman lived for many years, close to the center of Moscow. But Olga Mikhailovna [Grossman's wife] insisted — and stubbornly — on Novodevichye, the country's most prestigious cemetery. However, Lipkin added in January 1989 to the memoir that Grossman told both him and E.V. Zabolotskaya that he wanted to be buried in the Vostryakovo Jewish Cemetery. Lipkin's memoirs are unreliable in this regard. He even wrote that a Grossman's granite bust is there.

According to Fyodor Gruber, Olga Mikhailova's son, the Vagan'kovo cemetery was his mother's first choice, but her request was refused. The presented reason for the objection was that it was too soon to disturb the grave of his father who died eight years ago in 1956.

I believe that Olga Mikhailovna might have been glad by the Vagan'kovo cemetery management objections because she wanted the Novodevichye cemetery option. Nikolay Zabolotsky was buried there in 1958. Another famous poet Michael Svetlov recently died after being in the same hospital's ward just next to Grossman. This was completely justified vanity considerations of that circle of intellectuals in the authoritarian country prison who were born inside the walls without even filing them. However, the authorities knew better.

It would not be right now to judge people involved without completely understanding the circumstances at that time. However, the farewell ceremony and the arrangement for Grossman's ashes burial are now remarkable as a reflection of how the Soviet Union government treated Grossman even after his death. Lipkin described them in his memoir in detail.

It is a pity now that Grossman's grave is not at Vagan'kovo cemetery. Grossman wrote an essay like sketch Eternal Rest about Vagancovo cemetery between 1957-1960, in parallel with his main books. There are some traces of these books in the essay, for example, the most apparent: "' Everything flows, everything changes', said the Greek."

Grossman's bas-relief and his signature is on the headstone. The sculptor was Grossman's friend Pismenny's son.

 Grossman's daughter had found the Eternal Rest draft in an envelope while going through her father's papers. The essay was published only in Znamya magazine in May 1989.

The Grossman's grave is far away from the Begovay village at Troekurovskoe Cemetery. Irina Novikova, daughter-in-law (Fyodor's wife), had found the grave with some difficulty when Garrards wanted to visit it in 1990th.

A passage in Garrards' book about this visit:: "The grave selected to be a magnet for literary pilgrims is abandoned and unknown. The Jewish identity he claimed at the end of his life is absent on the headstone...His spirit enveloped us as we stood and contemplated his troubled life, and his final, posthumous triumph." (John & Carol Garrard, The Life and Fate of Vasily Grossman p .334).

Grossman is there alone out of the writers' community which abandoned him during his last years of life. When Russia comes to its senses and the country appreciates the prophet, Grossman's grave can be a place of penance and hope for a better life.

Suggestion

On this page, I would suggest a crazy idea of bringing together remnants of writers at a special place like the Volkovsky Cemetery's Literatorsky Mostky in Sant Petersburg. Transfer for re-burial (perezachoronenya) is a common practice. The Novodevichye Cemetery is prestigious, but let it leave for the authorities and their supporters. Writers have a different purpose in life. Grossman does not belong to the Novodevichye cemetery, the establishment vanity fair of the dead.

Vagan'kovskoye cemetery might be the right place. While facing Begovaya Village, it is close to Moscow Center, convenient for literary pilgrims.

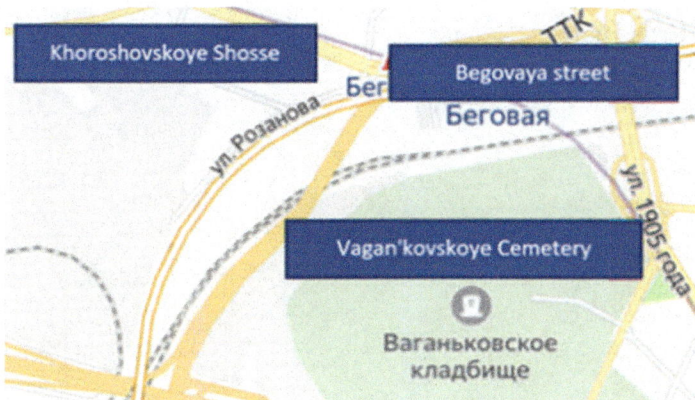

Khoroshovskoye Shosse — Begovaya street — Беговая — ул. Розанова — Бег — ТТК — ул. 1905 года — Vagan'kovskoye Cemetery — Ваганьковское кладбище

PART TWO

Vasily Grossman

Vas. Grossman

In contrast to Part One, which is predominately biographical and references-orientated, Part Two is concentrated on Vasily Grossman's literary work. It intends only to highlight the main books reflecting Grossman's development as a writer. These materials do not intend to make some critical research. Vas. Grossman is his pen name's designation, his signature. Not Vasily Grossman. Quotations from Vasily Grossman's books were published by the New York Review of Books unless mentioned otherwise.

The diagram presents Grossman's main books in approximate chronological order.

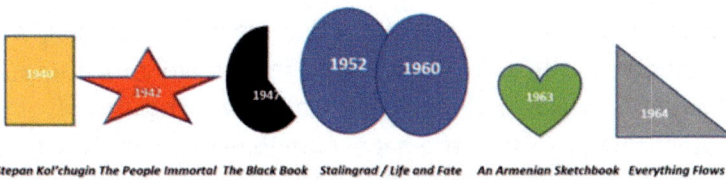

Stepan Kol'chugin The People Immortal The Black Book Stalingrad / Life and Fate An Armenian Sketchbook Everything Flows

Three distinct periods can be seen in Grossman's development as a writer in the diagram below: Soviet Russian writer in socialist realism mold before WWII; military writer during the war, and fiction writer in Russian classic literature tradition after the war.

Soviet Russian writer

Many writer's biographies include memories of early inclination for writing, especially poems. There is not any evidence of Grossman's literature experiments in early youth. He started to write during the late university chemical engineering studies. He wanted to work in political journalism.

Grossman comes into literature with an inherited sharp eye for details, including the psychology of people's behavior. His skills in the Russian language were also facilitated by his upbringing in secularized Jewish families. This cultural environment was genuinely absorbing the Russian language, sometimes to the native Russians understandable chagrin. The list of Jewish-speaking Russian language scholars and writers could fill the entire page. Additionally, from his both parents, Grossman was familiar not only with Russian classic literature but the best example of French fine literature.

Grossman arrived in Soviet literature as a product of communist ideology brainwashing, in our modern meaning of this definition. Despite his father's probable skepticism, Grossman was more than likely a true believer in the progress that brought a new life after the Bolsheviks' revolution.

Ordained by the founder of Soviet literature Maxim Gorky at that time only solely Russian classic literature representative, in the Soviet writers guild with the advice to follow writing should be truth rather than reflecting reality, the principle of so-called socialist realism, Grossman had not followed directly this advice but haven't gone apparently from the plow line. Grossman, by the way, jokingly in private called Gorky the founder.

Socialistic realism requires a writer to reflect life in its development in a positive direction with longing for a "positive heroic" character. Grossman's first novel Glückauf had been read and friendly criticized by Gorky just from this point. Socialist realism was formed as a rigid classicist architecture with numerous taboos and daring consequences for the writer to violate them. As a result, there was formed a kind of eclectic neoclassicism with baroque features.

The sad truth was that this production of the "engineers of human souls", as the Communist Party called writer, was consumed by the public as real literature. Grossman was a representative of this literature. The novel Stepan Kolchugin about a coalminer who became a revolutionary, established him in the realm of Soviet writers. He was accepted before in the Soviet Writer Union in 1937. After the publication of the Stepan Kolchugin duology, Grossman was in the first line of published soviet writers. Stepan Kol'chugin was published even by the children's literature publisher house "Detgiz."

Grossman perfectly fits with some adjustments to be a part of this type of literature. The fog of socialist realism occupied his head allowing him to produce literature work in this mold though marked with talent and skill.

I haven't read Glückauf in the Soviet Union and I could not get it now, but perhaps I would read it now with frustration. Stepan Kolchugin had not left in my memory anything from the time of my reading it in my school time. When I read this novel recently, I had only some anthropological interest, although the language was remarkable and some characters, like Stepan's mother, are memorable in the first part of the duology. The second part is boring. Grossman could not write the continuation not only the war interruption, but Stepan could not fit the post-revolution time. It would be a waste of time, in my view, the translation into English.

In his memoir, Ilya Ehrenburg wrote: "Grossman's first novel is his most Soviet, most social realist book. That doesn't mean it's bad. On the contrary, it has many good pages and episodes, there are subtle and well-written characters and storylines, this is elegant literature."

☐

Military writer

Grossman was considered a military writer in the Soviet Union and partially in the world. In my view, it is not right. He became nationally known as a writer on the front lines of WWII, but my main point is that the war experience changed his view of the country and he as a Jew is the subject of the presented materials.

The Soviet Union started preparation for an extension of the revolution throughout the world immediately after the short period of post-October Revolution recuperation. The Communist Party propaganda machine was concentrated on a militaristic set of minds in the population through movies, songs, and literature. Grossman entered the war as a fighter against fascism, at least in his literary work. We do not have any documentation of how sincere he was in this regard.

The military themes cannot be found in Grossman's work before the war, except for a few short stories. We do not have any traces of his attitude toward the Soviet army's "liberation" missions at the start of WWII in September 1939 and his intrusion into Finland in 1940.

War correspondent

After Germans broke the Nazi-Soviet agreement (Ribbentrop-Molotov pact) in June 1941, Grossman became the first rank journalist while working in the military newspaper *Red Star* (*Krasnaya Zvezda*) as captain- internal and ended his military service time as lieutenant colonel in Berlin. He was obliged to send correspondence articles to the newspaper twice a month.

His articles were in the mode of official propaganda. It would be right to say that they in general were similar to others, however, they included some substantial details that he could watch on the battlefield and after relentless communication with both commanders and different kinds of military, especially soldiers in the trenches. Reading Grossman's articles in the newspaper may be impressive because of his detailed knowledge of operations, which was, in general, understandable because he had access to information of high-level commanders, but among patriotic rhetoric, one can fill Grossman's knowledge of warier on the ground.

Both Iliya Ehrenburg and Grossman were the most popular journalists in the country. This was first-class military propaganda required by the country that fought a war on the border of life and death. While Ehrenburg first introduced the slogan "Kill the German", which was echoed by the poet Konstantin Simonov's poems, Grossman's reports appealed to the defenders.

While reading some of Grossman's articles in the *Red Star* newspaper, the soviet propaganda clichés are apparent. Actually, to Grossman's frustration, many lines could be inserted or demanded by the editorial staff. He complained about this to his father and wife letter.

Just some completely wrong examples are pure propaganda.

The German fascist "community" threw agriculture back 70-80 years. Again, there was a plow, a sickle, a chain, an antediluvian hand mill. Our state provided great assistance to collective farms with equipment, fuel, and loans. The fascists for two years of their rule did not give anything to the peasants of Kiev and Chernihiv regions. The plow and plow were dragged by peasants or harnessed cows and half-dead horses in them.

Grossman would not succumb to a concocted by Red Star's staff episode of 28 Panfil regiment group death during the Moscow battle. It became a propaganda banner for the entire country. However, at that time the country needed such literature. My father, wounded in 1942, remembered that Grossman was read with great interest. Grossman's adherence to the details of the war's truth made his writing so attractive that he had not noticed the propagandistic rhetoric that is so visible to a modern reader. We are not breathing the air of the war of that time.

Grossman kept notes which were published many years after his death. The book *Vasily Grossman A Writer at War: A Soviet Journalist with the Red Army*, 1941-1945 was published in 2007. See section A Writer at War in Appendices.

The People Immortal book

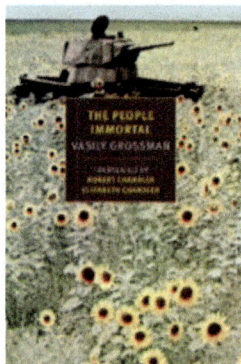

The People Immortal, Vasily Grossman. Translated by Robert Chandler & Elizabeth Chandler. Publisher New York Review of Books.

His book The People Immortal was written in 1942 before the Stalingrad battle. It was the first fiction book since the German-Soviet war break up. Sequences in 18 issues of the "Red Star", (Krasnaya Zvezda) military department newspaper. The 200-page novel was the first serious work of fiction in Soviet literature about the beginning of the war. Just reflected the need of people who defended the country on the front lines during the painful retreat after the German invasion.

Major-General David Yosifovich Ortenberg, editor-in-chief of the newspaper wrote: *'[After] precisely two months, Vasily Semyonovich brought me The People Immortal, a manuscript which was about two hundred pages long. I read it, so to speak, without putting it down. Nothing of the sort had been written since the war began. We decided to publish it without delay. The first chapter was sent to the typesetters. When the three-column page was ready, I started proofreading it. Grossman was standing by my side watching my movements jealously. He feared that I would make unnecessary corrections.'* Grossman, Vasily. A Writer at War (p. 114 Knopf Doubleday Publishing Group. Kindle Edition).

Reading today this book makes you uneasy. No, is this fiction book written by the same Grossman who *wrote Life and Fate*? Although there are some brilliant lines in the Russian language, the entire book is a propaganda pamphlet. Although the book is called *People Immortal*, the actual people are unremarkable, but the main heroes are commissars who looked as leading the military actions. By the way, later the army was restructured with emphasizing one commander in charge of diminishing the roles of commissars.

Most characters have Russian last names, just to put a flavor in the cocktail, an Armenian, as a representative of the Soviet Union. Although the events occurred in Ukraine, only a few Ukrainians are mentioned, a heroic old woman, a murdered chief of the collective farm, and a single old Ukrainian, Kotenko, who wanted to restore his farmland under Germans, and he hangs himself.

One negative personality is Lieutenant Mishansky, a typical Polish last name, mouse-like sounding. A deserter was shot in front of agreeing soldiers. They also suggested to kill a woman because the deserter stopped in her house.

As a propaganda tool, it was brilliant. Grossman established himself in the first line of official Soviet writers. Rumors were spread that he might receive Stalin's prize, which was not realized for unknown reasons. I read it now with definite shame for Grossman. But it is remarkable that in the book Years of War published in 1945, *The People Immortal* was included. In 1980, the collection of Grossman's work with the same title didn't have this piece. After *Life and Fate* Grossman, probably, would not publish it. However, the four volumes of Grossman's Russian publication included this novel in 1998. Yes, this is Grossman's war novel.

In a usually excellent Chandlers' translation, the book demonstrates the gap between Grossman at the beginning of WWII and the end of it. It was done on the assignment of the *Red Star* newspaper in 1942, before the Stalingrad battle. The language is excellent. The characters are memorable. All Soviet propaganda cliches are there, even a traitor carried understandable for a reader Polish name. Perhaps, the translation should not be done at all, leaving this small novel to professionals, who study Grossman, as a masterpiece of skillful Soviet propaganda. Unfortunately, it brings a wrong perception of Grossman. Just on 20th October 2022 in *Quadrant* magazine, a response appeared to *The People Immortal* English publication with a title "Vasily Grossman, the Man Who Loved War."

Holocaust materials

Grossman is completely justifiably considered one of the main Holocaust writers. Everywhere is written that his *The Hell of Treblinka* was an accusation document at the Nuremberg trial. He wrote special correspondence in the *Red Star*. However, these materials were not welcomed by the editorial staff and were heavily censored according to the official policies which went under the false slogan "Don't separate the dead." And *The Black Book's* publication fate became a scar on Grossman's soul.

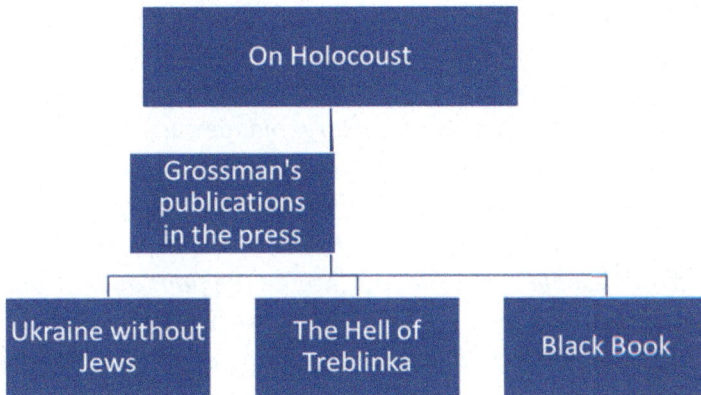

In the cities and villages of Poland, an article in the *Red Star* newspaper is an example of Grossman's correspondent work. Below is a long direct quote, which demonstrates Grossman style of these corresponds:

Nothing shows the monstrous essence of the fascist vampire as in national matters. The mass mechanized murder of Polish Jews took place over several years. People were told that they were being taken to labor camps, and then freight trains with doomed people were taken along the branch to special long low barracks. People were asked to undress and go to the "bathhouse". They were killed in these factories with carbon monoxide or electricity, and the bodies of those killed were burned in furnaces. One of these factories was located two kilometers from Lublin, and the second in the same area, at the Sabibur station, near Vladava. A Pole who had been in the trenches for a long time with a man who had fled from the Sabibur death factory told me such things that I don't have the strength to think or talk about it. This lies beyond all human notions of suffering and crime. This Pole also told that doomed, unarmed, naked people almost daily on the threshold of the factory entered the fight against the convoy and died the death of fighters. We have already written about the great epic of the struggle and death of the Warsaw ghetto. But now the strangulation of the Jews is over... The Sabibur Death Factory was moved to Kholm [city]. On the spot, her land was plowed, and wheat was sown. The most attentive person will not find traces of a monstrous massacre. But is it?

In the Kholm, since last year, fetid smoke has been billowing from a factory chimney. People told me that this smoke settled in an oily film in the larynx, and spiraled breath. For many days and nights, the Germans destroyed traces of another monstrous atrocity under the Hill. They burned the bodies of the Russian prisoners of war they had killed during 1941 and 1942. The bodies of the dead and tortured were buried, but when our offensive began last spring, the Sabibur Death Factory, having migrated to the Hill, began to burn tens of thousands of Russian prisoners of war killed by German villains.

The war brought also personal trauma as the extermination of Jews which led to his participation and later the most active editing of *The Black Book* and other writings on the Holocaust. It was the trigger for the next stage in Grossman's development as a writer that led to his adherence not only by form but also to the essence of Russian classic literature which was loosely defined as critical realism.

However, there was also a change in Grossman's personality. He started the war as a Jewish Russian and finished as a Russian Jew.

Jewish Russian War Russian Jew

Classic Russian literature writer

Grossman tried to be in the mold of Russian classic literature from the start of his work in fine literature. However, he had to go a thorny way to fulfill this intention under the condition of socialist realism main direction approved by the Soviet Union's ideological apparatus. He started his way in 1930th when this direction was introduced in 1932 and officially established during the first Soviet Writers Union congress in 1934.

Russian classic literature was not a separate island in the world's literature. Russian classic literature was in general accommodation in the Western intellectual tradition. Grossman contributed to fine literature river his work, which would flow forever until the world literature exists in the current form

Grossman always underlined that he as a writer is a follower of his forebears in Russian classic literature. Tolstoy's *War and Peace* was his permanent reading during the war. He suggested to a publishing house a study on Dostoevsky that was not supported because in the 50th   and even later was not in favor but the communist regime. Dostoevsky was treated as a reactionary writer. He had not been in school programs. A generation of soviet people was not aware of him.

I graduated the high school without reading any work of Dostoevsky in 1956. Dostoevsky Museum was opened in his former flat in Leningrad only in 1971.

Chekov was Grossman's favorite writer. He mentioned him in many of his works. The Bishop [Archirey] story was part of the subject of the characters' talks in the Life and Fate novel.

While *War and Piece* was written in the duology structure, Everything Flows and An Armenian Sketchbook is written more in traditional Russian classic literature second lines writers like Korolenko, Uspensky, Garshin, Grigorovich, and Kuprin. Russian classic literature giants were supported by many excellent writers which made it so powerful.

Grossman tried to fulfill his destiny to be a Russian classic writer. Leo Tolstoy, Fyodor Dostoevsky, and Anton Chekhov were Grossman's pillars in Russian classic literature.

As a continuation of Russian classical literature in the XX century, compositional unity is achieved by leitmotifs, repetitions of images, and different approaches to points of view. The compositional role of the plot is weakened in Vladimir Nabokov or Michail Bulgakov novels, especially in Grossman's friend Andrey Platonov's *The Foundation Pit or Chevengur*, but the sound and the ton of the Russian classic literature language remains.

Red Tolstoy

It is well known that the Communist Party leadership and Stalin himself wanted to have a literary fictional product to immortalize the war and the Stalingrad battle in a War and Pease like, a Red Tolstoy. Grossman was in the first line of the candidates. The bench of capable was small. Alexey Tolstoy was involved with an" assignment" to write about the Peter the Great novel. According to Grossman, Alexander Tvardovsky told him that the stunt reactionary and antisemite Mikhail Sholokhov (author of Quiet Don) once said: "I shan't myself be writing about Stalingrad, since it would be unacceptable to write worse than Grossman and I can't write better."

Stalingrad's novel imitates the structure of Leo Tolstoy's War and Peace through the Shaposhnikova family characters' lives and many subplots connected and even unrelated to the main plot. Like War and Peace, the novel includes immediate and perspective perceptions. One of the characters resembles Karataev, a self-made philosopher, and Ikonnikov., a former Tolstoian.

Two main lines are in Stalingrad's battle as a turning point of Soviet society as Grossman had seen it. During the war, the description of the everyday routine is more a camouflage of this basic Grossman's notion. Stalingrad battle was the real turning point in WWII. The military publication house Voenizdat wanted first to publish this novel because the narrative reflected real events in which Grossman was an active participant. Grossman even could communicate with many participants on the highest level.

An unexploded grenade was under his feet, he sailed in the Volga River under the artillery fire, he ate the same bread and drank the same water or vodka with participants of the battle. Of course, without the extreme hardship of the war, he saw and spoke to real people. Everything in Tolstoy's novel is his creative realistic imagination, in Grossman's everything is imprint. When he touches on German issues, he is not believable, it is more extrapolation from propaganda sources. He could talk to German prisoners, but this is not the same then the soldier was in his social environment. When he describes the soviet prison or camp without being there, the basic rules inside and outside the barbed wire are the same with the difference that in the prison the rule is applied to their extreme.

Grossman learned from Tolstoy that fiction which draws on history should not be necessarily historically accurate, but often is more powerful than precise history.

In the smaller pieces, like stories and essays, Grossman follows traditions of Russian classic literature. The story The Road just takes Tolstoy's The Strider: The Story of a Horse form in humanizing an Italian donkey.

Even in Stepan Kol'chugin one can feel Leo Tolstoy's hand by bringing an epic view to a local event or personal life. Ilia Ehrenburg wrote in his memoir: "Grossman's teacher was Leo Tolstoy. Vasily Semyonovich described the characters carefully, thoroughly, in long phrases, not being afraid of a lot of subordinate clauses ..."

Dostoevsky

Fyodor Dostoevsky attracts the modern reader by placing existentialism in a fine literature form. Grossman wrote Life and Fate when the term was already had been formulated. He placed in fine literature characters the basic ideas of freedom of choice your destiny under the hardship of war and the barbarian condition of a totalitarian state (Zenya-Krimov-Novikov line). Uncertain Zenya is a remembrance of Nastassja Filippovna who throws a pack of money in the fireplace-Dostoevsky novel Idiot. Aburchuk-Magur, Liss-Mostovoy, Krimov-Kancelebogen arguments, Viktor Shtrums dreams, Tea discussions in the Kazan group, and conversations with Chepyzhin resemble The Karamazov Brothers.

Finally, we get Grossman's philosophy of kindness as told by the "holy fool" Ikonnikov. Ikonnikov refuses his responsibility to slide under the guise of a deadly command structure and comes on for his freedom. This freedom is the source of the small goodness. It becomes manifest in the protest against the inevitable injustice. A few chapters later, the bed of Ikonnikov, who turns out to have been executed, is empty: "The holy fool? The man you used to call the blanc-mange? He was executed. He refused to work on the construction of an extermination camp. Keyze was ordered to shoot him" (*Life and Fate*, page 515).

Grossman brought up Dostoevsky, an almost forbidden name at that time the in Soviet Union conversation, although he was defined as a reactionary. Grossman proposed to do a study of Dostoevsky with no avail, as I already mentioned.

Chekhov

While remaining a genuine Soviet Russian writer, Grossman tried to follow the sharpness of Anton Chekhov's style of short writing. Archery story is part of the plot. Some chapters, especially in Life and Fate, are similar to Chekhov's short stories with the beginning and the end. Some chapters are Chekhov-style stories that live separately from the entire book, especially in Everything Flows (Mashen'ka Lubimova story). Chekhov's Heartache, talking to a horse, story, for example.

Chekhov was often mentioned in Life and Fate, including a special many-page discussion about Chekhov's democracy. In Life and Fate, Grossman wrote: "Chekhov lifted the failed Russian democracy on his shoulders. Chekhov's way is the birth of Russian freedom. We went the other way The Czechs introduced the whole community of Russia into our consciousness... Chekhov the standard-bearer himself the great banner that has been raised in Russia for thousands of years of its history, true, Russian, good Democracy... Russian human dignity, Russian freedom..." (Part One, chapter 64, pages 281-284).

As Robert Chandler, the Life and Fate translator, put it: "Life and Fate could perhaps be called a Chekhovian epic about human nature; like many great epics, it occasions ally shatters its frame."

In my amateur understanding, Ivan Bunin, Eugene Zamyatin, Michael Bulgakov, and Andrey Platonov moved ahead of the XIX century Russian classic literature into the XX century through different new forms. Grossman, while keeping the form of the XIX century, bringing the XX-century language, and addressing the same humanitarian philosophy of the XIX Russian classic literature, was a link to the extraordinary challenges of the XX century.

Jabotinsky

Vladimir Jabotinsky can be an exceptional example when a writer of Russian classical literature can combine, although already with elements of the modern Russian fin-de- siècle style, with political activities. We don't know how familiar Grossman was with him. At least, there is no evidence of it. However, if there was, it was not advertised because the "Lucky Grossman" knew that it was unsafe under those conditions, when Zionism, especially as the militants Jabotinsky's revisionist had been, was not only taboo, but also direct evidence of dissidence, and even a ticket for state actions. Grossman died earlier, but as a man fully familiar with the country and the regime, he could have foreseen. By the way, Jabotinsky, a brilliant stylist of the Russian language, wrote his books only in Russian. His family novel Five was never translated from Russian into English. His novel Samson the Nazarite was just about national self-identification and was Grossman's subject of the last literature work.

According to Alice Stone Nakchimovsky, "As the Jewish national movement blossomed in the 1960s and 1970s, his Russian-language legacy took on a second life…. Jabotinsky had come to age… His essays, written in still dazzling Russian, had a new appeal for Soviet Jews who far more than his generation were likely to share his sober of history." However, Jabotinsky died in 1940, before the Holocaust, which he relentlessly predicted, occurred in full-blown, and Grossman, who witnessed it, died before 1967 Israel's victory.

A personal observation about Russian classic literature value in the life of people in Russia, especially Jews. When the Gorbachev reforms had opened the gates out of the country for Jews, before leaving the country, they tried to send books to relatives. In Leningrad, long keys were formed on the main Post office, the only place for foreign parcels. There was a restriction that would not make sense to discuss here. People had sent Russian classic books that were on their home shelves. The bitter irony is that these books are not needed for their children and of course grandchildren. Sometimes, these books are placed on the street for free only to take them.

Grossman's literary work after WWII

Eternal Rest essay

Before starting to present the post-war main Grossman's works, I would like to place his less noticed, probably unfinished, *Eternal Rest* essay. It was written approximately 1957-1960 and published only in *Znamya* magazine in 1989. The essay was found by Grossman's daughter by accident in the form of separate pages. *Eternal Rest* essay is about the Moskow Vagankovo [pronounced Vagan'kovo] cemetery. According to Grossman's stepson, Grossman often went for walks in the cemetery where his father was buried in 1956.

The essay reflects on one of Grossman's disappointments as an internationalist because of his parents' upbringing and a person who had formed during the post-October Revolution time. It reflects Grossman's lounging for internationalism in the Soviet community immediately after the 1917 October Revolution. Even the French song L'Internationale became the anthem in 1918. It was replaced by the Hymn of the Soviet Union only during the war in 1944. As an example of the general internationalism attitude, propagated by the Communist Party's official policy, was the very popular verse *Grenada* written by Michel Svetlov (Scheinkman) about a Ukrainian soldier who *"left the house, Went to war, Land in Grenada Give to the peasants"*. The verse became lyrics for many songs, which were popular for years ahead.

Grossman treated 1934, the assassination of Sergey Kirov, as a turning point of the beginning of State terror which targeted, as he wrote at the end of the essay's narrative "the revolutionary intelligentsia, by workers with experience in the revolutionary underground", the predominately internationalistic Communist Party members.

He remarked that the tombs in the cemetery reflect intermarriages and the diversity of buried. He wrote with exclamation marks: *What a huge number of mixed marriages there were in those years! What wonderful equality between different nationalities! What a plethora of German, French, Italian, and English surnames! Some of the gravestones bear inscriptions in foreign languages. What a lot of Latvians, Jews, and Armenians!*

Grossman thought also of other nations in the restored Russian Empire under the name of the Soviet Union. After the Stalingrad battle, he was sent to Kalmykia. The fate of expelled during the war Kalmyks continued to reverberate with the possible fate of Jews before Stalin's death during the "Doctor's Plot". This essay had been written along with the *Life and Fate* novel where national identification was the central leitmotiv, first of all in the Jewish line. Grossman wrote: *"Stalin once said that the Soviet culture was Socialist in content and national in form. It proved, however, to be the other way around."*

Grossman's internationalism had not faded, but the humanistic line became dominant. The collection of short stories written after WWII was published in English under the title *The Road* in 2010. It includes such late stories as *The Elk*, *Mama*, *The Road*, *The Dog*, and *In Kislovodsk* with explicit humanistic content.

It is unclear why Grossman had not published the essay. Perhaps he hesitated to display such meditation on the interconnection between people alive and dead that reflects basic issues of life and death, that belong to poetry. Nevertheless, the essay is finished with a meditation on "the mystery of a human soul", which I want to place in the direct quote:

The sanctity of the souls' holy mystery makes everything else seem contemptible. The drums and the trumpets of the State, the wisdom of history, the stone of monuments, howls of loss, prayers of remembrance -- all this seems as nothing in the presence of this mystery.

My book *Jewish Journey of Vasily Grossman* starts with a Hasidic Rabbi David ben Solomon of Lelov (1746 –1813) adage *"The Jewish Journey is a journey to the root of the soul."*

☐

Stalingrad (For a Just Cause) novel

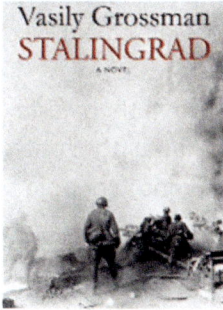

Overshadowed by *Life and Fate*, the *Stalingrad* part of the duology is the best example of Grossman's writing style in the tradition of Russian classic literature. Let's go to some details of this novel as an example of Grossman's development as a writer and a person. In contrast with *Life and Fate*, it is less known to the general public. Stalingrad is closer to the traditions of Russian classical literature by the structure of the novel's design. This section aims to show that Grossman is a genuine part of this trend in world literature.

Stalingrad (For a Just Cause) was an attempt to insert socialist realism in the form of Russian classic literature. Grossman became a sort of a "classic" in soviet literature, at least he was in the first line of published soviet writers. However, the fine literature realism could not fit the form. The novel is filled with flesh of memorable characters and episodes from Grossman's life and war correspondent experience. From today's hindsight, Grossman might be glad he distanced himself from many places.

The novel was originally called *Stalingrad* by Grossman. It was changed by the editors with Grossman's consent. It resembled Vyacheslav Molotov's announcement on June 21, 1941, about the outbreak of the war with Germany: "Our cause is just, we will win." Although the title translation in English *For the Right Cause* sounds more assertive than *For a Just Cause*, Grossman wrote about the Stalingrad battle, one of the turning points of the war, as a turning point in people's personal lives and the government itself. The For a Just Cause title is commonly accepted and correct, in my view.

Stalingrad's novel publishing history

Stalingrad's publishing ordeal is the case study of mostly unsuccessful attempts to tear the shackles of socialist realism. Stalingrad's publishing history is even more remarkable than Life and Fate's as a reflection of intellectual life at the time when Grossman worked. The story of the novel's publication can be interesting to read by itself as a non-fiction document of the suffocating atmosphere of life for intellectuals. There are nine variants of the novel damaged by editors, censors, and self-censorship. Even Grossman himself insincerely admitted his so-called ideological errors. In 1949, Voenizdat released in the form of pamphlets excerpts from the novel entitled: "On the Volga. (Chapters from the novel 'Stalingrad').

Finishing the novel Grossman gave it to one of the main "tick" magazine's Znamya (editor-in-chief Vadim Kozhevnikov) in 1948. During the war, Grossman had good working relationships with this magazine. But in the spring of 1949, he transferred the manuscript to another prominent magazine Novy Mir after Konstantin Simonov took over the mazarine's editor-in-chief. Simonov worked as a correspondent for Red Star newspaper during the war. He replaced Grossman in Stalingrad. In 1950, Alexander Tvardovsky, Grossman's close friend, became the magazine's editor-in-chief. The names of the magazine' editors-in-chief are mentioned because they were decisive players in the novel's publishing ordeal. It took three years for the novel's publication.

The diagram reflects highlights of the *Stalingrad/For a Just Cause* publishing story in the *Novy Mir* magazine. It is described in detail in Popoff's biography book in the chapter A Soviet Tolstoy (pp.196-212). It is worth reading as a description of the suffocating atmosphere of Grossman's working space, the idiocy of demands for publication, and the painful compromises that are required to see the book published. Grossman maintained a diary of the publication course (The Diary of the Manuscript's Progress).

This book, the novel is called "For a Just Cause", by the way.

Fall 1949	Winter 1950	Spring 1950	Summer 1950	1951	Summer 1952
Simonov proposed to downplay the Jewish theme, take out Shtrum	Tvardovsky agreed to publish only the war parts.	Grossman received proofs after extensive multiple revisions.	Publication was suspended. The manuscript was sent for the Party's Central Committee approval.	The manuscript was substantially revised under guidance of the Writer's Union's chief Fadeev.	The novel was published in four subsequent (July-October) issues.

After the Novy Mir publication, the novel had enthusiastic support from readers. Two publishing houses, Voenisdat (military literature publication) and Sovieskij Pisatel' (The Writer's Union publication) completed the right to print a book. The Voenizdat paid advance money. Then came the January 1953, "Doctor's Plot" that followed the secret trial of the Jewish Anti-Fascist Committee (FAC). The Sovieskij Pisatel' harshly criticized the book's Jewish theme. Voenizdat requested the return of the advance. Tvardovsky held a denouncement meeting in the Novy Mir magazine office.

In February, an array of articles appeared in newspapers assaulting Grossman for his novel's nationalistic mistakes. On March 2, three days before Stalin's death was pronaoses, the *Novy Mir*'s editorial board published a statement in the *Literary Gazette* (*Literaturnaya Gazeta*) where the publishing of the novel was "a grave mistake." At the same time, Fadeev summoned the denouncement Writer's Union meeting to condemn Grossman for the novel. Even in March, already when Stalin was in the Mausoleum, the *Literaturnaya Gazeta* editor Simonov published Fadeev's repentance for the novel's publication.

There is a notion, supported by some friendly to Grossman literary critics, that Stalingrad is for reading only once. Levin, would you like to read it again? I agree and disagree. On one hand, rereading would only for fast perusal to remind the characters which appeared in Life and Fate or to enjoy again some excellent piece of prose, forgiving the rhetoric which might be imposed by editors and Grossman agreed to save the entire novel during stormy days of the novel publication.

On the other hand, while rereading For a Just Cause, one can be impressed with the power of the writing, for example, the description of the Stalingrad fire, the battle at Stalingrad rail station, the death of Filyashkin's battalion, the meeting of major Berezkin with his wife belong to the best pages of Russian prose; the last pages of the meeting love scene cannot be read without approaching a lump in the throat. The Shaposhnikovs line is better in Stalingrad than in Life and Fate. The Kovalev Lena Gnatuk chapters are moving. And the end of Lena's life in the pit: A high-explosive bomb fell in the pit where Lena Gnatyuk and two orderlies were caring for the wounded. Every last breath of life was cut short. (p.898). The translation does not give the filling of deep sorrow.
Grossman placed in the same sentence intentionally, starting with an "and."

In Stalingrad is the seed that becomes a tree. After you read Stalingrad with different eyes. Reread the family gathering. You cannot understand the end of LF without knowing Tamara Bereskin from the fire in the beginning and in Stalingrad's miraculous meeting with her husband their love song in the night together and the final pages in Life and Fate during their walk breathing the Spring air.

In Stalingrad, the main disappointment during and after the war: was fissures that became visible between his acceptance of himself as a Jewish Russian and Russin Jew.

Some critics, for example, Alexander Solzhenitsyn's nitpicking in a 2003 review, are useless because this is a novel but not a war correspondence in a newspaper. Most readers would not care while enjoying the rhythm of the prose narrative.

Who cares about the construction of windmills in Don Quixote? More difficult is to be cooped up with ideological rhetoric. However, besides the censors, publishers, and editors, they reflect Grossman's true convictions at that time. He believed in Marxism (his father was a Menshevik) and even Leninism. To some extent, perhaps Grossman's attitude toward Stalin was not negative during the war. He thought that bloodshed during the war would clean up Stalin's war crimes. Later he admitted his dilution, that is in Life and Fate and other following works.

Many pages in *Stalingrad* can be read by a modern person with uneasiness. For example, hard communist Krymov's thoughts.

"Rarely in his life the essence of Soviet unity so clear to him" Or " And all those random memories, sudden, fleeting the thoughts that arose united around the big and important, the most important and significant. The party sent the difficult work of a man Spiridonov knew, a party man, comrade, Bolshevik".

Or "The party organized battalions, regiments, divisions! The party organized the military-industrial power of the country! The Party admonished its sons with words of truth, as harsh as life itself."

We cannot how much faith in victory in these "words of truth" was inserted on the editor's demand. Some socialistic realism cartoonish characters like the miner Novikov make the reading frustrating.

However, at that time this book was accepted with enthusiasm as a breath of fresh air. An excerpt from a letter to Grossman by a military writer Victor Nekrasov: "For the past four months, I've been looking forward to the release of each new issue of *Novy Mir*.

 And it's not just me. My friends are fighting - who can get the latest books of the magazine from me first. I still haven't met a person who wouldn't be happy about the appearance of your novel.

 The Death of the Battalion is done so well that I can't even find words to convey all the feelings that I had when I read this piece. In its strength, truthfulness, severity, and simplicity, this is a piece that I do not know is equal to all military literature. And not only this piece..."

The Jewish line was the main sticking point which had been objected to by the non-nonce ideological watchdogs of the totalitarian regime. The guards at the gates of the regime were not asleep.

Grossman was accused of Zionism. They demanded to take out Shtrum. Grossman was not only a war correspondent but hardened during the war. He did not surrender Shtrum. Grossman stood fast while agreeing on 12 reductions, even apparently unrealistic about the role of political instruction before the battles. Due to the editorial mutilations, there are different variants even the published first part of the duology. There are three very different publications during Grossman's life (1952, 1954, and 1956). Remarkable, one of them is almost "Judenfrei" except the name Shtrum.

Additional remarks.

The English edition of the *Stalingrad* novel published in Robert and Elizabeth translation is from the 1956 variant. It includes the same fragments omitted in the 1952 and 1954 variants by the editors' requests. The English edition has many useful features about Viktor Shtrum: careful and detailed notes in the afterword about 1952, 1954, and 1956 variants, maps, and a very useful list of main characters.

Life and Fate novel

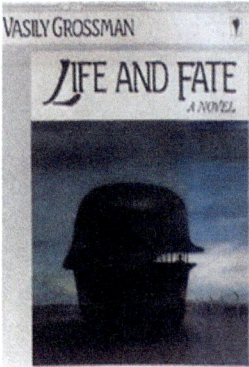

Life and Fate, his magnum opus, is read, treated, and studied as a political statement and philosophical meditation that it is in general true, but the underlying background story is the love for people, whose life and place is destroyed. This novel is studied and continues to be a subject for different kinds of research that these materials do not even try to be a part. These materials only reflect my perception of the book.

Publication ordeal

The dramatic ordeal of *the Life and Fate* manuscript publication will stay in the annals of world literature. There is the famous " sentence: Manuscripts don't burn" in Michael Bulgakov's novel *Master and Margarita*.

The diagram of its publication might be useful as just a remainder. It is well known, although there is still today some confusion about its tracks.

Oktober 1960	December 19, 1960	January 5, 1961	February 14, 1961	February 26,1962	July 23,1962
Delivered to *Znamya* magazine	Editorial board meeting	Publication rejected	Manuscript arrested by KGB	The letter to Khrushchev	Meeting with Suslov

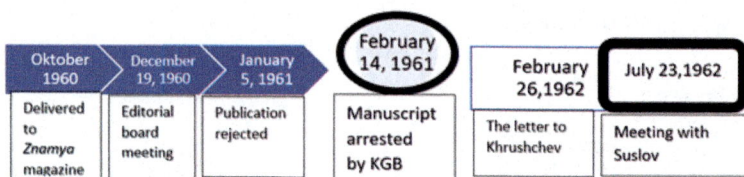

Before his death, Grossman made the last arrangements to hide the manuscript. As a final result, the manuscript was saved and published in Switzerland in 1980,16 years later. See Part One *Life and Fate* catastrophe).

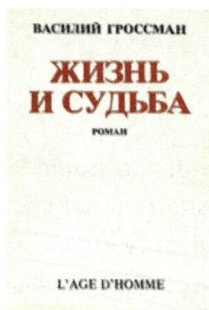

ВАСИЛИЙ ГРОССМАН

ЖИЗНЬ И СУДЬБА

роман

L'AGE D'HOMME

The first publication of Life and Fate in Russian by the Swiss private publication house L'AGE D'HOMME.

Stalingrad vs. *Life and Fate* or *Stalingrad + Life and Fate*

Life and Fate only technically occurs in the fall of 1942- spring of 1943, but in reality, it is the postwar life devastation, definitely during the doctor's plot time, postwar party purges Leningrad, Slansky, Cold War, Grossman considered as different novels not only without censorship and perhaps less self-censorship damages, although the novel was written for publication. Grossman certaily knew the allowed limits.

Stalingrad is an introductory novel to *Life and Fate*. The two novels are connected by characters, time, and the place of events. Although they are very different, without the first, the second-line characters' actions cannot be understood. They are different only as a person of different ages. A young adult with still illusions and maturity with disappointments still with hopes. The novels are inseparable.

Grossman had in Life and Fate sequence a chance to say what he wanted to say in Stalingrad when he wrote with his hands tied with the mouth gag. We cannot dismiss the danger to his life and family.

However, Grossman avoided calling a sequel to Stalingrad. In 1960, in No. 21 of the newspaper "Soviet Warrior", he wrote: "... I finished a large multifaceted novel "Life and Fate". Working on it for about ten years. There are many characters in this book, known to readers from the novel "For a Just Cause" (Lydia Chukovskaya Notes about Anna Akhmatova. V.2 YMCA-Press, Paris, 1980, p. 601). According to Grossman's friend Natalia Roskina: "Vasily Semyonovich [Grossman] believes that "Life and Fate' is an independent thing, although it is connected with the first book."

The duology is one book not only by characters but by the principle of the narrative. Stalingrad can be viewed as an opera's overture. All main themes are presented there except the Jewish line. It was only in some troubling notes.

If we clear Stalingrad of many propaganda shells which were a tribute to editors, censors, and self-censorship, Stalingrad does not have the socialist realism feature in the depiction of events and characters as presenting them in the perspective of the socialistic way of development, which is in the canon of socialist realism.

Without Stalingrad, many characters are paling in Life and Fate. For example, the Abarchuk's, former Ludmila Nicolaevna Shaposhnikov's husband line. In Stalingrad, Major Ivan Beryozkin and his wife Tamara had met by accident near Stalingrad's suburb Kamishin. Their talk there during the night is Grossman's jewel of a love song. Their walk in the last episode of Life and Fate is crucial for the entire meaning of the duology. And Serezha Shaposhnikov in the House 6/9 cannot be understood without Stalingrad's novel. Son of a Russian Dmitry Nikolayevich and a Jew Ida Semyonovna. Both perished in the GULAG. Serezha was sent out from the 6/1 house by Grekov who, in his words, "fought for freedom" there. If Serezha had survived the war, he might end up as a dissident with his critical thinking. Most of the dissidents were Jews in the Soviet Union. A Jew by Halakha, maybe he will end up in Israel.

Without the *"They"* episode in the bomb shelter in Stalingrad, Boris Korol's episode in Life and Fate does not have its meaning of "bloodless" antisemitism. *"Nina affair"* and Grossman's struggle with the Mother's Letter can not be understood. Other examples can be shown.

Song on Love book

Stalingrad is a book on war. The war destroyed Stalingrad's city and lives. *Stalingrad* ended up with uncertainties in war (commissar Krymov crossed the Volga River before the Stalingrad battle was won). *Life and Fate* is saturated with love stories during the war. Krymov wept after three days of torture receiving a parcel with the signed "Your Genya." Stepan Fyodrovich Spiridonov, who lost his beloved wife Maria Nicolaevna, drowning in the Volga, experienced just born love for Natalya. Sereza Shaposhnikow and Kathya' love anf life were saved for now by "House 6/9 manager" Grekov. *Life and Fate's* last pages end with a love story (Berezkin meets his wife Tamara again, but now not by accident as in *Stalingrad*. They are standing in silence holding hands breathing the air of Spring) Berezkin, now the lieutenant colonel, and Tamara, are not even mentioned. Only those who have read the Stalingrad novel can recognize them because they are a metaphor. Tamara whispered in the night: "It's my love that kept you alive."

One book writer

World literature usually selects, often unfairly, one book for common use as a classic. *Decameron* Bocaccio, *Devine Comedy* Dante, *Don Quixote* Cervantes, even *Faust* Goethe.

Without going into literature research exercises In Russian classic literature despite some competing no less remarkable books, for the general public in the West, the most popular Tolstoy is known as *War and Peace*, Dostoevsky *Crime and Punishment*.

Grossman's Stalingrad/Life and Fate accumulated all written by him while contributing to their specific way different sides of his fine literature works.

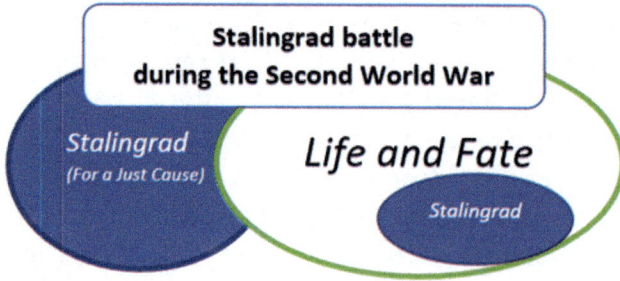

.

Duology metaphors

As a great writer, Grossman placed many of his thoughts and notions in episodes as metaphors. They are disseminated through the duology, concentrating them in *Life and Fate* for many reasons, but predominantly because they are related to the Jewish throughline in the novel. For this reason, they are presented in detail and I have placed direct quotes from the novels in my book Jewish Journey of Vasily Grossman.

Because these metaphors would not fit the current biography requiring a separate publication like a book, here is only the list of them with pages from the original text *Stalingrad* and *Life and Fate* New York Review of Books (NYRB) publication and my *Jewish Journey of Vasily Grossman* (JJVG) on Amazon books publication.
The hidden hope is that perhaps these excerpts would be an impetus to read the entire duology. I am here accompanying the metaphors with my interpretation of them with apparent simplification and approximate evaluation.

These metaphors require a special research study that is out of the scope of this biographical book and a professional approach which I apparently cannot provide.

Two episodes of the first city bombing chapter in *Stalingrad's* novel -"They", the Jews- street antisemitism [page 586 (NYRB); page 50 (JJVG)].
The enamel brooch- internationalism [pages548, 585- 586 (NYRB); pages 51-53(JJVG)].

"Nina affair" episode, page350 (NYRB) pages 123-127(JJVG)
The Mother's letter - betrayal of Jews [p358-359 ages(NYRB) ;124 (JJVG).

Life and Fate episodes

Sofya Levinton- Jewish and humans Motherhood [page 544-554 (NYRB); pages 64-65(JJVG).

 Soviet and German soldiers in one blast crater –
internationalism
House 6/1 metaphor of freedom Grekov to Krymov:
' Freedom. That's I'm fighting for.' [page 427 (NYRB)].
Revolutions devour their children metaphor in Stalingrad false premise.

Flight squadron episode of "bloodless" antisemitism [pages 85-88 (JJVG); 167-170; (NYRB)].

 Genocidal antisemitism in the Natasha Karasik episode[pages 200; 203-204(NYRB) ; 91-92(JJVG]

Unfinished duology

Neither final variant manuscripts of Stalingrad nor Fate and Life exist. Stalingrad is almost fatally damaged by editors, self-censorship, and compliance to be published as a way to make a living according to his family's standard of life. Although in the 1956 edition, Grossman tried to fix something, Grossman wrote everything that he could at this particular time. The dead are gone. We are left with complete uncertainty about the fate of the characters.

Life and Fate also had been written still with a hope to be published in that environment. The variant had been left at the stage or before the arrest with the minimal reader and without just professional friendly editors who always are necessary as the additional pair of eyes. Just one example, in *Life and Fate*, Natasha could not sing in a cattle wagon because she lived in the Jewish ghetto.

Both novels are now at the mercy of opinions with different knowledge and often agendas that follow the current approaches. Grossman might have a different understanding which is important perhaps more than current as an immediate experience. Even if they were proven wrong, they are valuable for our future generation of readers. High-level classic literature gives a concentrated snapshot of the time that remains. We do not read newspapers or even memories to judge the 19th century but rather Madam Bovary or Anna Karenina.

Robert Chandler, the translator into English, took the third 1956 variant of Stalingrad for translation into English after comparing it with other versions. Published in Russian in 1998 under the management of S.I. Lipkin is less complete. At first sight, the 1956 variant was published when Grossman was alive. However, the Agitprop machine was in full power. It is doubtful that Grossman could fight it being interested in publishing according to official editorial and censorship demands. Editors were also censors by default.

There was enormous resistance to discussing the Holocaust after the war, especially before Stalin's death when antisemitism returned in force. The official Soviet narrative was that everyone had suffered equally during the war. Grossman hoped to use fiction form to tell some uncomfortable truths. Probably, he hoped that it would have to pass muster with the censors. A noticeable narrative device used by him was to present minor, socially marginal characters to express the harshest critiques. This allowed him to formally distance himself from those views.

Hopefully, someday, a consensus committee will arrange a more or less final edition of both novels as one edition. *Stalingrad* especially needs an abridged variant to omit in general irrelevant to the spirit of duology and make it less intimidating by the amount pages of pure socialist realism can be omitted without any damage to the book. Some military descriptions valuable to the main publisher Voenizdat (Military Publishing house) are also relevant to generals and other military persons at the time of the book writing, but now and especially for the future reader completely a thunderstorm of yesterday's rain.

What is the duology about? I'm taking the liberty to present my view of reading and rereading this book. Again, this is one book which is divided into two voluminous novels.

It is about people's betrayal after they won on the fields of Stalingrad. Stalin defeated Hitler. Red Army outmaneuver Wehrmacht. The Soviet Union had enormous people resources, but Hitler had unreliable allay, the Rumanian flank that made it possible to encircle Paulus 6 army. But the battle was won by the 62 army where Fedjashkins battalions and Grekov's 6/1 homes were completely gone, while Berezkins miraculously survived. But it was only the beginning of the spring of 1943 and we do not know their fate after.

People's lives were destroyed on every level from Shaposhnikov to Novikov and Krymov. They were connected by Zenya Shaposhnikova. Even if Novikov had not involuntary betrayed Krymov, the Getmanovs and Neudobnovs won after the war and actually during the war by official Russian chauvinism.

In the 1960 article written in memory of extraordinary Russian writer Andrey Platonov, Grossman said: "*The fame of the writer is not always in full accordance with his actual meaning and true place in literature. Time is the attorney general in cases of undeserved fame. But time is not an enemy to the true values of literature, but a reasonable and good friend to them, a calm and faithful guardian of them.*"

Some pages are just poems in prose. The final 870-71 pages where *the light instead of tinkling and gurgling, it was like a soft cloak swathed round the earth.* And other lines that cannot be translated as real poetry.

I am unsure that had *Life and Fate* been published when it was written, it would have been understood and completely appreciated by society. I remember myself and my surroundings at that time. However, in the epochal times of the 21st century, I am convinced only Grossman will be read as a mirror of the social explosions in the 20th century.

Only Grossman is relevant now during the war that the Russian Federation (I'm reluctant to use Russia) imposed on Ukraine. Among the second half of 20th century Russian writers, Vasily Grossman is mentioned often. Michal Bulgakov or Isaak Babel rarely because they belong to the first half of the 20th century , before the WWII. Neither Boris Pasternak nor Aleksandr Solzhenitsyn are interesting now. The latter is with his "How can we equip Russia", more to point at a wrong way.

Just on a panel discussion on November 12, 2022, in Kyiv, a person in the chat placed a message about *Life and Fate.* The five participants knew the novel, and one of them remarked that 60 years before Grossman anticipated Ruscism, a Russian variant of fascism. Now this term is only at the level of scholars, politicians, and publicists to describe the political ideology and social practices of the Russian state in the late 20th and early 21st centuries, as well as supporters of Russian military aggression against Ukraine.

Wall Street Journal journalist Evan Gershkovish, wrongly accused of espionage, read *Life and Fate* in Russian Prison in 2023.

Everything Flows ... novelette

In my view, *Everything Flows...* and *An Armenian Sketchbook* while being separate literary works in the form of a small novel and a traveler's notes, besides their targeted purpose, can be read as footnotes to Life and Fate on social (*Everything Flows...*) and nationality (*An American Sketchbook*) issues. Let's go to these books.

History of publication

Grossman started *Everything Flows...* in parallel with Life and Fate approximately in 1955. The Stalingrad publication ordeal was over. He made corrections to it in 1956 to restore some pages that were cut in the *Novi Mir's* magazine publication. Correctly anticipating that *Everything Flows...* is unpublishable, he worked on it to the end of his life in 1964. Grossman had read some chapters to friends. His wife and stepson worried about the danger of this reckless behavior in their mind.

The novel was printed by Russian emigrant publisher house Posev in (Frankfurt am Main) in 1970. Two chapters (7th and 14th) were printed earlier in the same year, 1970) in Frankfurt magazine Grani, No78. The novel was released in 1971 in Italian by Milan publishing house "Mondadori"; in 1972 - in English by New York Publishers Harper & Rowe; in French (Paris publishing house, "Stock"; in Serbian by Belgrade publishing house 'Obelisk'; in 1975 - in Hebrew by Tel Aviv publisher Am Oved; in 1977 - in Swedish by Stockholm forum publishing house.

Until today it is not known who smuggled the manuscript to the West. At that time nobody would admit it, but now it does not matter. An uproar of criticism immediately occurred from both sides. Russian emigrants blamed Grossman for Russophobia. Vladimir Maximov, the editor of the Paris-based Russian journal *Kontinent*, has defined Grossman's reflections on Russian history as an "openly racist declaration." Soviet authorities accused Grossman posthumously for anti-Soviet and other sins. Luckily, Grossman did not know this unfair reception of his book. He was already dead six years ago. Grossman had liked Russians and was a patriot of his country though with reservations. He wanted to heal it from apparent sins.

In *An Armenian Sketchbook*, Grossman tried to clarify this issue arguing in advance years after he died in 1964. Moreover, Grossman underlines the positive influence of Russian cultural influence on multiple different nations of the former Russian Empire. It seems that he was sincere. The Soviet Union, with all its damage to these nations in general, was in line with these positive tendencies.

The cold and even negative attitude toward *Everything Flows...* in the Russian emigrant publishing community might influenced the delay of *Life and Fate* publication from the smuggled abroad manuscript. The attention and discussion of it among intellectuals in the West were artificially delayed. Time was lost. More details about this controversy are in Y. Bit-Yunan and D. Feldman's book *Vasily Grossman Biography on the political content in the Soviet Union.*

In The Soviet Union, *Everything Flows...* was published for the first time in the Oktyabr magazine in 1989, one year after *Life and Fate* and two years before the name of the country disappeared from the world map. The publication was an intellectual event among the country's reading population. The magazine accompanied the publication of the novel with an article by philosopher G. Vodovozov entitled "Lenin and Stalin", which was almost one-third of the novel by size. There was no Grossman's alleged Russophobia mentioned.

The book came to Soviet Union readers too late. People were busy in search of food from gradually emptied grocery stores. After Gorbachev's failed anti-alcohol policy, special talons were issued on vodka, quite a popular consumption product in the country.

Political pamphlet in the fiction form

As Grossman wrote Lenin's and Stalin's destructive for Russia work continued after their death, the legacy of the USSR still lingering. Grossman's bitter thoughts are echoed in the disastrous wars that its successor, the Russian Federation, carried on after its dissolution. However, the aim of these pages is only to discuss that Grossman follows the traditions of Russian classic literature in Everything Flows book.

Everything Flows... book looks like a finished small novel or a large story, but to me, this piece is a sketch loosely combined by the main character, Ivan Grigoryevich. In my reading, Everything Flows... is an unfinished and never-be-finished draft for Life and Fate. Both are farewell declarations with Soviet literature and joining with Russian classic literature.

Reading after *Life and Fate*, *Everything Flows*... looks pale. It appears more as a political pamphlet. However, it is not right. Brilliant entering chapter in the train which brings a slate of the country unknown to Ivan Grigoryevich. *Everything Flows*... continues one of the main Life and Fate lines of the country's betrayals of the people who stood fast when a foreign power intruded. Grossman added in his last days the essay about Judas. It is a multilayer reflection of people's nature, but the country consists of people who willingly or urgently commit betrayal by circumstances.

Four types of Judas pamphlet like insert looks satirical and lightweight element in it, but in admitting one's guilt, in repentance, the author, the Soviet writer Grossman, participated in everything, both glorious and shameful. He indeed is ashamed and grave not for the informers only, but also for himself, for his former enthusiasm, myopia worked to the end of his life.

The included separate stories underline Grossman's general thoughts. Everything Flows is continuing the same style of *War and Peace*. The narrative where everyday life chores descriptions are interrupted by general life issues.

A different country

Ivan Grigoryevich returned to a different country. He was a stranger in the Khabarovsk Express, in Moscow and Leningrad. *"There were no house no well, - only a few stones shinning white amid dusty grass that had been burned by the sun"* when he traveled to his hometown where his father's house was.

Everything Flows... in contrast to *Life and Fate* is not Grossman's book of repentance. Ivan Grigoryevich regrets his lost life when the country betrayed him and his country's people. He came to motherhood as a prodigal son, but he stood upright, "yet still the same as ever, unchanged "in his longing for personal freedom and the defense of his dignity, as Grossman himself. *Everything Flows...* emphasizes the humanistic part of life, while *An Armenian Sketchbook* is devoted to people's nationality identity.

My *Everything Flows...* adventure

Perhaps, these memory notes would be appropriate in this book because they show why Grossman came to his reading audience so late. Generation missed Grossman to its detriment.

Verboten books, which were printed abroad and somehow brought into the Soviet Union, had started to move around. Grossman's Everything Flows... was the first piece of illegal literature that my friend and I photographed for distribution among our circle of friends in Leningrad in the early 80th. We worked in an anatomical pathology department in a hospital. We had a minuscule photo laboratory that was allowed by the nature of our professional work. The principle was simple. We received a copy of the book from a trusted friend. We did one set of negative films late in the evening when nobody was in the department, of course, without notifying anyone, including our wives. After a long old-fashioned procedure of printing on photo papers, the negative film was burned. The book was returned with a box of printed copies. The copies should not be returned. In the same way, we did other "tamizdat" (printed abroad books). We were unhappy, even frustrated when sometimes our production came back to us. With the hindsight of many years, I'm wondering how reckless this enterprise for adults was. We were not dissidents. Now, I suspect that the books could be intentionally implanted by the 5th KGB department to follow potential illegal activity chains without touching the benign fools. Eventually, the creak of books dried out safely for all participants as far as I am aware.

An Armenian Sketchbook

An Armenian Sketchbook, Vasily Grossman's last large piece of finished work, which is sometimes called a memoir, travelog, or travel sketch. Initially, the manuscript was called Travel Notes by a Man of Advanced Years. Grossman changed the title to DOBRO VAM! (I Wish You Well!), a translation from the Armenian Barev dzes, a greeting and farewell by the Armenians. The subtitle is *From Travelers Notes.*

Despite numerous studies on Grossman's legacy, including periodically published editions of the Grossman Studies Center in Italy, Turin, *An Armenian Sketchbook* has not received the attention it deserves. This book is the pinnacle of Grossman's writing skills. □

The publication fate of *An Armenian Sketchbook*

An Armenian Sketchbook was written during 1962–1963, immediately upon Grossman's return from Armenia, where he had finalized his translation of a war novel The Children of the Large House by Hrachya Kochar from Armenian to Russian.

The trip occurred eight months after his Life and Fate novel had been confiscated on February 14th, 1961. Although a volume of already-published stories came out in 1962, and four new stories appeared in periodicals between June 1962 and September 1964, Grossman needed a respite from the suffocating Moscow air.

Grossman brought the manuscript to the *Novy Mir*, the most respected, so-called "thick" magazine in the country. The magazine's editor-in-chief was Alexander Tvardovsky, a close family friend of his. Tvardovsky was the main player in all dramatic adventures with the *Stalingrad's* novel publication.

An Armenian Sketchbook was not published during Grossman's lifetime. According to Semyon Lipkin, Grossman's friend, who published his memoir *Life and Fate of Vasily Grossman* in 1989, the commonly accepted reason was his stubbornness to remove, on the demand of a censor, a 12-line paragraph about Jews at a wedding in a village in Armenia. However, Lipkin's statement contradicts the actual edited manuscript, in which actually Tvardovsky objects to the paragraph. The details were presented in investigative research by Yury Bit-Yunan in Russia in 2020.

Now, it does not matter who objected to this paragraph, but perhaps, at the time when these events occurred, it mattered to Grossman. If the censor objected, it would be more acceptable to Grossman because it was how society was designed, and he spent his entire life as a writer self-censoring. Glavlit, the censoring body, gives the undisputable final verdict like a sunset. Respect for Tvardovsky was so high that Glavlit might not have noticed or pretended to overlook some troubling Jewish insertions among completely benign travel memoir chatter.

Another thing for Grossman might be when Tvardovsky objected as a matter of self-gardening over preconsciousness to touch the Jewish theme too much. Tvardovsky, from his side, left enough "unkosher" materials, and this paragraph looked too "treif, no kosher" Tvardovsky wrote in his diary: "Bull! Why do you need to ask for things that I don't believe in?" He was probably offended and frustrated that Grossman was unthankful for his effort to save the book. He was aware more than Grossman of the winds that had flown from the Communist Party leadership because he had direct contact with them. Tvardovsky did not want to fight for Grossman. At that time, he tried to convince Nikita Khrushchev to allow the publication of Alexander Solzhenitsyn's *One Day in the Life of Ivan Denisovich* story. The fate of *An Armenian Sketchbook* being published was predestined to failure.

A bizarre episode related to the memoir's publication is worth mentioning because it illustrated the authorities wrought toward Grossman's writings. Grossman's old friend Anna Samoylovna Berser facilitated the publication of a chapter about Sevan Lake, a completely benign piece, in the weekend very popular at that time magazine *Nedelya.* She had connections with the editor-in-chief Aleksey Adgubey, Khrushchev's son-in-law. Grossman was excited to break the silence around him with this publication, really a literature jewel. The piece was already in print for the Moscow edition, however, in the middle of the printing, the deputy of the editor came in, stopped the print, and replaced it with a different material. The authorities continued to fight with the writer on his deathbed.

This event was remarkable as a reflection of the intellectual air in the country. The tragic sign was not that a watchdog of the regime or self-preserving editor could object to a completely benign text, but that even Grossman's friends wanted to tolerate this knife stabbing and manipulation in the wound. Members of his family surely disapproved of his stubbornness. But Grossman knew better.

The Russian language magazine *Literaturnaya Armenia* published the manuscript in 1965 almost a year after Grossman's death. The book Dobro Vam! the title of Grossman's manuscript, was published among some other stories in Moscow in 1967, omitting some of its chapters. The full text was published only in 1988 (Znamya magazine #11).

The title

An Armenian Sketchbook is called sometimes a memoir (Alexandra Popov in her book Vasily Grossman and the Soviet Century,) or travelog, or travel sketch.

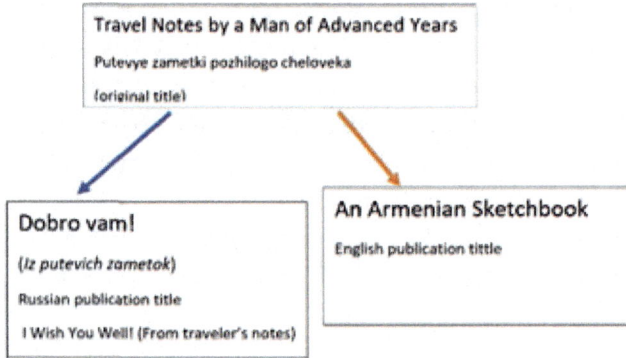

Travel Notes by a Man of Advanced Years

Putevye zametki pozhilogo cheloveka

(original title)

Dobro vam!

(*Iz putevich zametok*)

Russian publication title

I Wish You Well! (From traveler's notes)

An Armenian Sketchbook

English publication tittle

It would not be a great revelation to the statement that the title is a crucial part of the writer's piece. In the Novy Mir magazine submission, Grossman changed the original title for translation from Armenian Barev dzes, a greeting and farewell by the Armenians. Not health as Russians do, but well-being—I Wish You Well! Grossman's wish to humans. But he placed the subtitle to make the title less pompous, as just some remarks, and notes.

Why would not be right to go with the original title in the translation into English? The translators (Robert and Elizabeth Chandler) deserve the highest marks for everything that they did for Grossman's popularization in the West, but the change of the title is unfortunate despite the extraordinary quality of the translation. However, publishers know, perhaps, better for a book distribution on the market.

Grossman convoluted his secret thoughts in two forms: naturalistically personal, even human physiology, most fictional, but necessary to sneak in the people's yards, homes, and trams, and fictional, like his Armenian writer-employer Martirosyan and the translator Hortensia. Everything was fictitious except the stones, churches, roads, mountains, lakes, and some people whom he met and some events like trips to a restaurant, to Vazgen I, and of course the wedding. As a great writer, he filled the Armenian landscape, with gray dead stones and flourishing flowers, with people and animals, alive and dead, but part of life that was his subject of interest. The trip to Armenia was for him a fate's gift to concentrate his thoughts about people's historical evolution through thousands of years.

The Poem in prose

An Armenian Sketchbook is a poem. My statement is far from original. Many readers noticed this. Some writers and literature critics have called the book a poem in prose. It is so obvious that it would be completely justified if the word poem would be placed instead of The Traveler's Notes, as Grossman initially placed it as a title for this book. It is written in "I" form which is not the usual form for Grossman. It is about people. In this situation, he would be the person most familiar to him.

Grossman placed human study in the form of a poem in prose. I believe that he always was a poet but ashamed to write verses and wrote self-controlled prose. In the last piece, *An Armenia Sketchbook*, this control has somehow weakened.

Unfortunately, the translation could not transfer the poetic part. Reading aloud some pages sounds like a poem. Especially in Chapter 11 about faith and churches. The chapter on Sevan Lake stands out as a mixture of poetry, self-deprecating irony, and satiric indictment of the regime. Any translation is not able to deliver the rhythm of sentences, specific use of words, or cultural hints. Russian free word order fights with the sentence construction in English, but that brings a special rhythm.

The poetic flavor disappears very much in the translation because it is specific to a Russian speaker's word use and associations with them. Completely acceptable in Russian, in English they look awkward. Sometimes the translator simply omits them unable to find a similar equivalent. Some cultural landmark requires a note of clarification even for a modern Russian speaker, but the poetry spirit disappears.

The translation is correct but the rhythm of word sequence is lost. It is only text. In Тяжелого, жестокого, ужасного the sound of the Ж letter is lost. The English alphabet's consonants do not have hissing sounds. I don't think that Grossman intentionally collected this sequence of letters. It comes from the subconscious as a real poet does in opposite to people who are able for versification, as most are able, but not a real poet.

Just an example of untranslatable poetry.

This white blossom is the expression of the water of the forest, an expression of the half-dark of the forest, of the vague outlines of plants lying deep in the water, of the way silent white clouds slide over this water, of the reflection in it of the crescent moon and the stars. And all this—streams, backwaters, forest ponds, and lakes, rushes and sedges, sunrises, and sunsets, rustling leaves and reeds, the sound of air bubbling up to the surface, the strange, lonely sighs from the silt—all this finds its expression in the white water lily. And in the same way, the world of modest female beauty finds its expression in Astra. As for what may lie hidden in the depths of these waters, no one can say unless he breaks the water's smooth surface, walks barefoot through the cutting sedge, and treads the silty, sucking mud—now cold, now strangely warm. (p. 43).

Like in real poetry, while rereading, you open something unseen or unheard when the swamp or a sheep looks at you. There is in An Armenian Sketchbook a certain rhythm of chapters, there are rhymes of repetitions to deliver the main thoughts (Rachell Semyonovna traveled there….).

I would take the liberty to suggest that *An Armenian Sketchbook* is a kind of a sonnet in prose. It is finished like a sonnet with a 12th chapter punch scene, which made the piece unpublishable during Grossman's life.

Summary of Vas. Grossman as a Soviet Russian classic writer

At this point, I am stopping my presentation of Grossman as a representative of Russian classic literature.

Who was Vas. Grossman (the pen name of Yosif Solomonovich Grossman)?

Working as a professional writer in the Soviet Union during the darkest time of this country's history, Grossman followed the best traditions of classic Russian literature. He was closer to Anton Chekov by the style of writing, while Fyodor Dostoevsky attracted him by philosophical and psychological depth.

The Second World War, which occurred in the most dramatic way after Germany's invasion of the Soviet Union in 1941, required besides military and industrial effort, intellectual support for propaganda purposes. One of them was planned by the ideological part of the Communist Party apparatus to develop a major epopee, kind of John Galsworthy's *The Forsyte Saga*, but of course, something similar to Leo Tolstoy's *War and Peace*. They needed a Red Tolstoy.

As the most prominent correspondent and already the author of the first book about the war, *The People Immortal*, Grossman was a natural candidate to facilitate such a task. Ordinated by the Union of Soviet Writer, one of the branches of the Communist Party propaganda machine, Grossman started this task in 1943.

.

Appendices

Vasily Grossman's books in English

Translated into English, Vasily Grossman's books are placed in chronological sequence from the first publication.

There are two translations into English of the same book: by Thomas P. Whitney titled *Forever Flowing* in 1972 and with a title *Everything Flows...* by Robert and Elizabeth Chandler in 2009. All citations are from the Chandlers' translation.

Words of gratitude to Robert Chandler and Elizabeth Chandler for their relentless translations of Vasily Grossman's literary work. Their careful maintenance of the spirit of the Russian language is amazing. Formulated in English, the meaning of Grossman's thoughts sometimes looks more impressive.

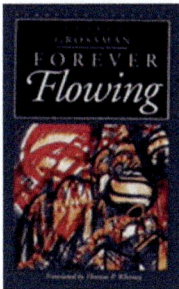

1972 Forever Flowing

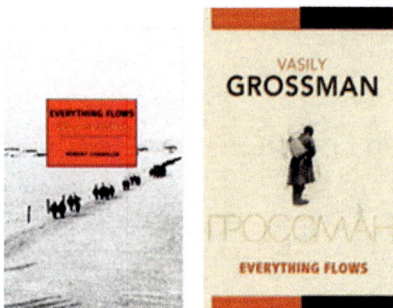

2009 USA   2010 UK

Everything Flows...

Published by the New York Review of Books in 2009. Robert Chandler under the title Everything Flows...

In my view, the *Everything Flows...* title reflects more precisely the meaning of Grossman's book than *Forever Flowing.*

Everything flows is the first part of Heraclitus's dictum "Everything flows, everything changes..." as one of the basic postulates of dialectic. Turned into a short-winged phrase, Grossman used this it on some occasions.

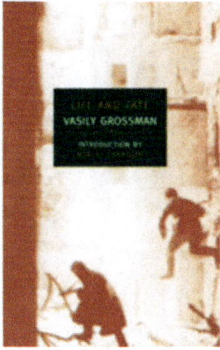

1985 Life and Fate

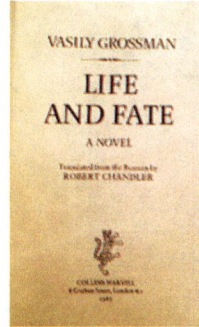

Published by the New York Review of Books. Translated with an introduction by Robert Chandler. On the right, 1985 Collins and Harvill UK publication.

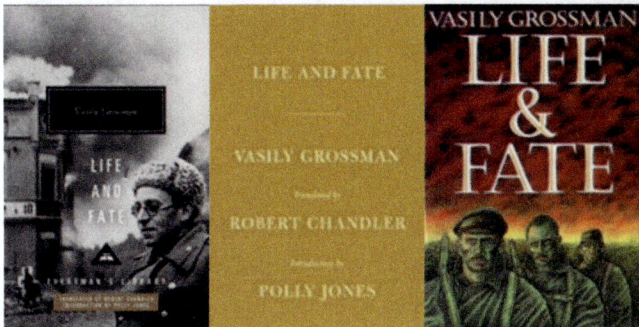

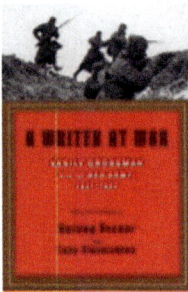

2005 A Writer At War Vasily Grossman with the Red Army 1941-1945. Published by the Harvell Press. Edited and translated by Anthony Beever & Luba Vinogradova.

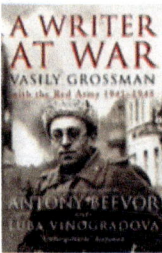

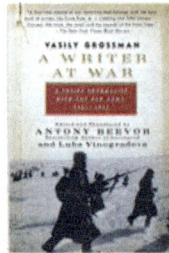

2007 Vintage Books   2006 UK Pimlico

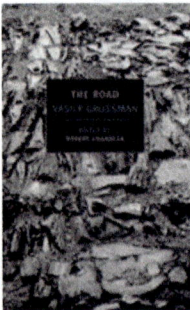

2010 The Road New York Review of Books. Translated by Robert and Elizabeth Chandler with Olga Mukovnikova.

2013 An Armenian Sketchbook Translated by Robert and Elizabeth Chandler.

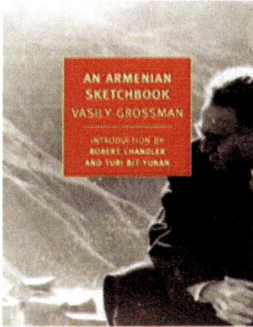

New York Review of Books   Quercus MacLehose Press

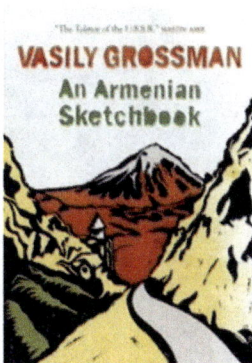

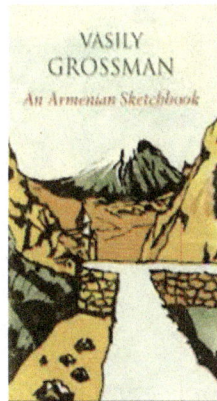

2019 Stalingrad Translated by Robert and Elizabeth Chandler

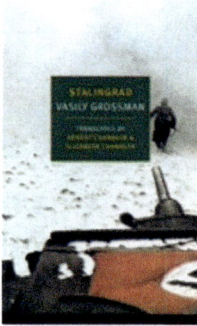

New York Review of Books USA   Harvill Secker UK

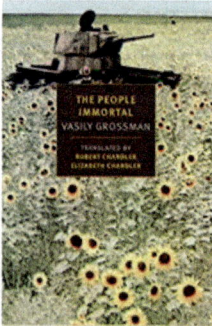

2022 The People Immortal Translated by Robert and Elizabeth Chandler.

New York Review of Books

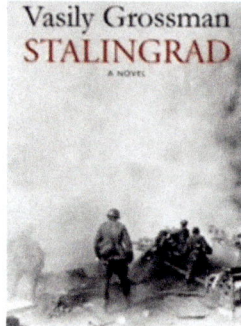

References

The References title of this section is not completely accurate because it gives the wrong impression that these materials might look like an academic study that is not in line with the spirit and design of this book. I prefer to consider them as part of an extended essay. The books presented below are in my possession. I've read and quoted them. Some materials are available only online.

Books

Literature devoted to the Jewish theme is scarce, especially books. The main book on the Jewish theme is still Shimon Markish's *The Vasily Grossman's Example* published in 1985 in Israel. As far as I am aware, there is only one book on this subject, only in Russian. The book is in two volumes: the first one includes excerpts from Grossman's books, and the second is about the Jewish theme in them. Shimon Markish called his work a sketch. It was quoted on many occasions in the current book.

Vassily Grossman
Selected Works

ו. גרוסמן
מוטיבים יהודיים

The Example of V.Grossman
by Sh.Markish

ש. מרקיש
דוגמתו של ו. גרוסמן

Vasily Grossman (Le cas Grossman [The Grossman Case] in French, 1983.

Shimon Markish (1931–2003) was a classical scholar and
translator.
His father, the Soviet poet Peretz Markish was arrested in
1949 and executed in 1952, one of the thirteen Soviet Jews
on the "Night of the Murdered Poets."

Shimon Markish left the Soviet Union in 1970. He worked as
a scholar of classic literature at the Department of Russian in
Geneva for 22 years. Markish wrote essays and books on
major Russian-Jewish writers Isaak Babel, Ilya Ehrenburg, and
Vasily Grossman.

**Shimon Markish and Efim Etkind facilitated the publication
of the *Life and Fate* novel (Lausanne, 1980).**

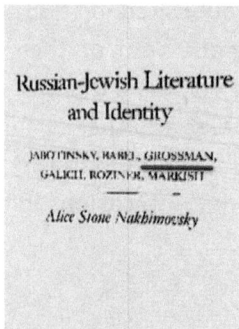

Russian-Jewish Literature
and Identity

JABOTINSKY, BABEL, GROSSMAN,
GALICH, ROZINER, MARKISH

Alice Stone Nakhimovsky

Alise Stone Nakhimosky's *Russian-Jewish Literature and
Identity* book was written under the auspices of the Johns
Hopkins Jewish Studies program. Published in 1992, this book
includes chapters on writers of Jewish descent who wrote in
Russian: Vladimir Jabotinsky, Isaak Babel, Vasily Grossman,
Aleksandr Galich, Felix Roziner, and David Markish. Two
chapters were devoted to Grossman.

Nina Henrixovna Elina (1916 – 2007) Vasily Grossman
Jerusalem1994; Jews in world literature seria. Ithe
Grossman's biography. In the Russian language, The main
books retailed, as well as S. Lipkin's memoir book. In her
book, Nina Elina stated that the Jewish theme sounded in
Grossman, sometimes albeit muted, but always and
invariably.

Boris Frezinsky's 2009 book *Mosaic of Jewish Fate. XX
century*, who wrote in the chapter Big Man Grossman:
" These two books were written by the same talented and
honest man, but two different writers – a Soviet writer and a
free writer. Grossman's Soviet books had a difficult
publishing fate, but this only helped the writer to choose
freedom."

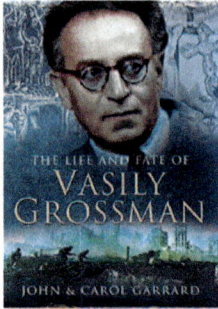

The Life and Fate of Vasily Grossman by John Garrard and Carol Garrard. *Pen & Sward* Military, 2012. Copyright Study Center Vasily Grossman.

First published under the title *The Bones of Berdichev* in the USA in 1996 by The Free Press.

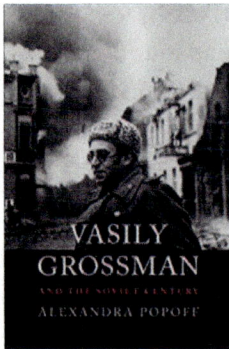

Vasily Grossman and the Soviet Century by Alexandra Popoff. 2019 Yale University Press.

Overview: If Vasily Grossman's 1961 masterpiece, Life and Fate, had been published during his lifetime, it would have reached the world together with Pasternak's Doctor Zhivago and before Solzhenitsyn's Gulag. But Life and Fate was seized by the KGB. When it emerged posthumously, decades later, it was recognized as the War and Peace of the twentieth century.

Biography publications in Russian

Yuriy Bit-Yunan, David Feldman: *Vasily Grossman in the mirror of literary intrigue*s Moskva. Forum; Neolit, 2016.

Annotation: V.S. Grossman is one of the most famous Russian writers of the XX century. In the pre-war and post-war years, he found himself in the epicenter of literary and political intrigues, miraculously avoiding arrest. In 1961, the manuscripts of the novel "Life and Fate" were confiscated by the KGB by order of the Central Committee of the CPSU. A quarter of a century later, when the book published abroad was translated into European languages, world fame came. However, intrigues in connection with the writer's legacy continued. Now not only Soviet. Authors reconstruct the biography of the writer, simultaneously eliminating the already established "myths". In the preparation of the publication, documents of the Russian State Archive of Literature and Art, the Russian State Archive of Social and Political History, the Central Archive of the Federal Security Service were used.

*Vasiliĭ Grossman : literaturnai͡a ˘biografii͡a ˘v istoriko-
politicheskom kontekste* [Vasily Grossman: literary biography
in the historic-political context] Authors: David Feldman,
Yuriy Bit-Yunan. Publisher Litres, 2020.

Annotation:

"A new book "Vasily Grossman. Literary Biography in the
Historical and Political Context" continues the monograph by
Yuri Bit-Yunan and David Feldman, dedicated to the life of
the famous writer. The authors reconstruct the biography of
Grossman, "simultaneously eliminating already established
myths."

I am in debt to the honorable Yuriy Bit Yunan for providing
me with a Word file of this book.

Unavailable now, for the sake of completeness, Anatoly
Bocharov's first Grossman biography *"Vasily Grossman: Life,
Work, Fate* (1990, 402 pages pdf 2,9 MB, in Russian).

Memoirs, articles, letters

Introductory words

Memoirs about Grossman are relatively few, bearing in mind that interest in his work and character continues today. Remarkably, the interest is not related to the dates of this birth or death, but to events. For example, the war in Ukraine generated an explosion of articles in the periodical press.

Memoirs have one peculiar particularity in that they were written around 20 years after Grossman died. There is a reason for this, but it is not right to analyze without knowing the details of that environment and the particular details in each case.

Most common is the admiration for Grossman's character. Naturally, it is the degree of resistance to the temptation to bring the memoirist to be a part of Grossman's life.

 All memoirs are written in Russian. There is not any translation in English. For this reason, some extended quotations from them would be right to place, but the space does not allow me to do it. placed.

My comments on the memoirs' materials are made with a certain restraint, however, it would not be right to omit them, although the scientific analysis of them had been done by Yuriy Bit-Yanan and David Feldman's publications.

Books

Lipkin Semyon Izraelevich was Grossman's long-time close friend who left most of the memoir literature. All of Grossman's biographers quote Lipkin's books and other memorial statements. As already mentioned, Yury Bit-Yunan and David Feldman's publications provide a critical analysis of Lipkin's memoirs. However, it is indisputable, that Grossman considered Lipkin as his trusted friend as can be seen from his letters to him. During one of the most troubling times in the winter of 1953 when the apogee of the antisemitic campaign was in whole swing during the "Doctor's Plot", Grossman was "hiding" with Lipkin near Moscow.

Семен ЛИПКИН
ЖИЗНЬ
И СУДЬБА
Василия
ГРОССМАНА

Анна БЕРЗЕР
ПРОЩАНИЕ

МОСКВА-КНИГА-1990

1984   1990

The first Lipkin's memoir was published in 1974 and then added with a preface in 1984. The memoir had a title *Stalingrad Vasiliya Grossmana* [*Stalingrad of Vasily Grossman*] In 1990, Lipkin published a memoir *Life and Fate of Vasily Grossman*, which included the previous book published in 1984. This was a combined publication with Anna Berser's book *Farewell*.

Berser Anna Samoylovna (1917– 1994), was a long-time editor of Novy Mir magazine and Grossman's personal friend. The book Farewell is distinguished for its description of the last days of Grossman's life in the hospital when Berser took turns with Grossman's wife and Ekaterina Vasilievna Zabolotskaya. According to Berser, she was at the last Grossman's day, although according to Fyodor Gruber's memoir book on the last night of Vasily Grossman's life, Efim Abramovich Kugel was on duty at his bedside. Her memory pages are passionate.

Roskina Natalia Alexandrovna (1927 – 1989) author of numerous publications on Russian literature, specialist in A.P. Chekhov and A.S. Suvorin.

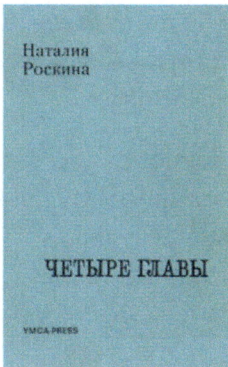

Четыре главы

Четыре главы (Paris: YMCA, 1980. The book includes four memoir chapters. The third chapter is called In Memory of Grossman (pp101-129).

Guber Fyodor Borisovich (1931-2020)

Memory and Letters. The Book about Vasily Grossman
(Fyodor Guber, Pamiat' i pis'ma (Moscow: Probel, 2007), in
Russian. The book belongs to Grossman's stepson, Olga
Michailovna Guber, Grossman's second wife.

From the Annotation: The book contains much of what I have
remembered over nearly three decades of my life alongside
Grossman, to whom I have been a son all these years. It is
called "Memory and Letters" since what is not reflected in
the letters of the writer or letters to him is presented in the
book from memory. The peculiarity of this book is the large
number of letters used and the usually small volume of
fragments given from them: what I could tell about the
events of the life of Vasily Grossman in my own words, the
writer himself, and other participants in these events will tell
incomparably brighter and more convincingly.

The book includes some childhood memories. It presents
some of Grossman's preferences in music, poetry, and fine
literature. Also, there are memories of Grossman's friends
and protagonists of characters in Grossman's books related
to family members.

According to Yuriy Bit-Yunan's research studies, the access to
the Central Literature archive to Grossman's family archive,
including those documents that were preserved by
Zabolotskaya, was closed for a long time at the request of
Fyodor Guber. Since 1988, he has published materials in
periodicals.

Articles

Shimon Markish published three articles *A Russian Writer's Jewish Fate* (April 198)6 in the conservative Jewish magazine Commentary, an influential publication among intellectuals in the 1960s-1980s. His first name is printed as Simon. In this name, he was called in Russian.

The last article is in high degree the translation of the Example of Vasily Grossman's second book from Russian into English.

Shimon Markish's conclusion about Grossman, as a writer after the Second World War, reflects such quote from the article: "But, although Jewish fate shaped and sculpted him, this new writer, he remains a Russian writer – a Russian writer of Jewish destiny."

Yampolsky Boris Samoylovich (1912–1972), The last meeting with Grossman, (Posledniaia vstrecha s Vasiliem Grossmanom,) Kontinent, no. 8 (1976), p. 140. "Kontinent" was a Russian literary, journalistic, and religious magazine, published from 1974 to 1992 in Paris

Zaks Boris Germanovich (1908-1998) A Little about Grossman (Nemnogo o Grossmane), Kontinent, №26,стр. 355).

Taratuta Yevgenia Alexandrovna (1912-2005) "Chestnaia zhizn' i tiazhkaia sud'ba: Vospominania o Vasilii Grossmane," Ogonyok, no. 40 (1987): 22–23.

Druzhnikov Yuri.Vasily Grossman's Lessons. Memory Pages. (In Russian). 2001.Chaika (1) magazine.

Remarks about Grossman's letters

In Grossman's case, the correspondence is incomplete, selectively presented, and even redacted.

Fyodor Guber, Grossman's stepson, limited access to them. In his book *Memory and Letters* (the book about Vasily Grossman), he presented them selectively. The same can be said about Lipkin's representation of the letters.

However, the letters, which are still available, are full of Grossman's personality and he compensates for the minimal humor in his novel and other writing, except the last *An Armenian Sketchbook*, with hidden allusions that require knowledge of their background. Reading them is a pleasure.

They are sometimes over-affectionate, which in communication would sound superfluous, but appropriate in a letter, to establish a connection with the addressee.

"Two hundred years" *Life and Fate* publication delay controversy

The memoirs section, perhaps, would be an appropriate place to touch on some controversies in Grossman's ordeal with Life and Fate publication, omitting the Stalin prize awards and bugging his apartment issues. In this regard, the Yiriy Bit-Yunan study provides some data based on research. I am going to refer to this study because it gives a clue on the reliability of memoirists in general and in this issue in particular.

One of the most frequently quoted elements is that Mikhail Suslov, the chief Kremlin ideologue, told Grossman in June 1962 that there was no question of Life and Fate being published for at least two hundred years. Suslov made notes beforehand which have now been published. They contain no "two hundred years."

In Bit-Yunan opinion, "The "two hundred years" story also seems to have developed only gradually; it seems to have been engendered by the writer Boris Yampolsky, to have been helped on its way by Roskina, and then — once again — to have been more widely disseminated by Lipkin.

Grossman compiled a long and detailed record of the conversation as soon as he returned home. The record does not mention this. In my belief, keeping in mind the Communist Party's school of restrain in the expression of their thought, he could make such assertions.

"Krymov complex"
Some introductory personal remarks

Artur Koestler's *Darkness at Noon* novel was for me the trigger to return to Grossman. The silly adventure with illegal "samizdat" copying *Everything Flows...* was described in the introduction to the novelette on page 96.

The second part of 1980th is defined as Gorbachev's "perestroika" turbulent time. A flood of books, prose and poetry, and other previously verboten materials were published in many so-called "thick" literary journals. People, including our family, collected them in self-made binding books. Among them was the translation of Arthur Koestler's *Darkness at Noon*. That time was not suitable for reading due to the necessity of doing everyday chores under conditions of lack of food in stores and preparation for emigration. The book didn't impress me at that time.

Much later, in the USA, I returned to it following an article about Koestler by Algis Valigunas in *Commentary* magazine. I've read both variants in English and Russian. One thing that caught my attention was that the main character's, Nicolas Rubashov, Jewish identity was intentionally hidden by Koestler. I published an essay *"Revealed in Translation"* about this subject in the *Moment* magazine in 2014. The excellent novel translation into Russian by Andrei Kistyakovsky made it more impressive. The translation filled the novel with an air of reality. Still, in my view, *Darkness at Noon* is incomparable with *Life and Fate* masterpiece. But they were written at different times by different writer skill authors. Koestler's mastery of English had only just begun.

"Krymov complex" vs. "Rubashov complex"

Nikolay Krymov in *Stalingrad/Life and Fate* duology and Nicolas Rubashov in *Darkness at Noon*.

Shimon Markish suggested that the "Krymov complex" has many more rights to terminological dignity than the long-ago entered in literature the "Rubashov complex" term named after the hero of Koestler's *Darkness at Noon* novel. Markish wrote that for him Nikolai Krymov's suffering and insights in prison seem to be the pinnacle of Grossman's psychologism when he described stages of Krymov's development from a powerful arrogant Bolshevik to a crushed person who was in tears receiving a letter in the KGB jail from abandoned him ex-wife, Eugenia Nilolaevna (Zhenia} Shaposhnikova ("Your Zhenia" note at the end of the letter).

The suggested by Shimon Markish "Krymov complex" includes different forms of the revolutionaries' self-destruction and realization of it. The "Krymov complex" is broader than a reflection on self-inflicted wound damage. It assumes different stages of its realization. "Rubashov complex" is just a variant of it. It is remarkable to see the evolution of the "Rubashov complex" Rubashov kept some hope by writing the "Theory of Relative Maturity" project. *Darkness at Noon* was written before WWII in 1939.

In my reading, Rubashov, as a literary character, looks pale compared to Krymov in Grossman's duology, but together they create a portrait of people who set the world on fire and eventually were crushed by monsters in the very movements they participated in developing.

Revolutions devour their children

The near truism of the 18th-century adage that the revolutions eat their people, the allusion to Saturn, the Greek myth of a titan who ate his children, has numerous confirmations in history. The Russian October Revolution was not an exception.

Grossman presents an array of characters in the duology that reflect the "Krymov complex": Abarchuk with Magar, Katselenbogen, and Mostovoy in between. They represent examples of how the revolution consumes and digests its perpetrators. The main is, of course, Nikolay Krymov.

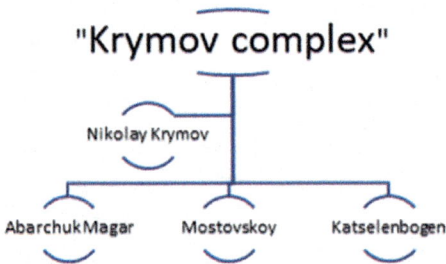

"Krymov complex"

Nikolay Krymov

Abarchuk Magar   Mostovskoy   Katselenbogen

Grossman has a different attitude toward them. He shows a great deal of sympathy with Krymov. Grossman himself was willingly a cog in the Communist Party propaganda machine by circumstances of war. The fate of Nikolay Krymov's character is a part of Vasily Grossman's remorse. Viktor Shtrum is also part of the "Krymov complex", as Grosman himself. The duology protagonists haven't survived, while Shtrum/Grossman was wounded, but able to leave us the duology for thinking about life and the fate of our mistakes.

Krymov

The last 56 sections of 961 pages of the *Stalingrad* novel sentence sound as *"But Krymov was now in a grip of the new impressions; he was walking on the earth of Stalingrad."* After crossing the Volga River in a flippy boat under German fire, Krymov moved to the final stage of his life which can be defined as "Krymov Complex".

Krymov left behind the pinnacle of his life achievement when "With him, under his leadership, were 200 soldiers and commanders whom he had met on his way" by foot out of encirclement by German troops. *"There were moments afterward when Krymov felt I he must have dreamed this entire journey..."* page 274. ..." *sense of responsibility was the source of Krymov's strength. Dozens, hundreds of times every day men turned to him with the words "Comrade Commissar!" (page 276")...*"When Krymov looked around at his troops , staggering from weakness yet still a force to be reckoned with, he felt both pride and joy".*(Page 280). "Rarely in his life had the essence of Soviet unity seemed so clear to him... Krymov's life had taken shape in a world of Communist ideals; more than that, it was woven from these ideals." (Page 290.)

However, when *he was walking on the earth of Stalingrad,* reaching the House 6/1 with lectures on politics and international affairs, his words fell on deaf ears. Nobody needed his Communist propaganda on this island of people, where the "house - manager" Captain Grekov answered Krymov's question: *'What do you want?'* *'Freedom. That's what I'm fighting for.'* (page 427).

The entire conversation between them is filled with many remarkable nuances which require special analysis. The Krymov's visit 6/1 house "adventure" ended up suspiciously unusual " *That night, while he was asleep, Krymov was hit in the head by a stray bullet...A sudden thought flashed through Krymov's head. Maybe it was Grekov who had shot him*? (page 429).

Remarkably, Grekov had sent out from the 6/1 house Seryozha Shaposhnikov. Grossman did not want to meet this open-minded young man with his uncle-in-law.

6/1/ house was the starting point of the "Krymov complex" which formed in the KGB prison where Krymov was placed after a bogus denunciation as a hidden supporter of Trotsky and the enemy of the State. Herein the Lubyanka prison *"Sometimes Krymov himself began to doubt"*. He remembered that *"He had denounced Grekov to the Political Administration of the Front. If it hadn't been for the German bombs, Grekov would have been shot in front of other officers."*

The "Krymov complex" was developed by Nikolay Krymov in its entirety during interrogations and *Evenings in a hut near the Lubyanka* . . .(A black humor allusion to *Evenings on a Farm Near Dikanka* a collection of short funny stories by Nikolai Gogol) *Krymov was lying on his bunk after being interrogated – groaning, thinking and talking to Katsenelenbogen* (p. 841).

Like Nilolas Rubashov in Arthur Koestler's *Darkness at Noon*, Nikolay Krymov was interrogated by two KGB officers, soft and crude. They were different from Rubashov's, less intelligent and more vulgar, just rude and offensive. Time was different. *Darkness at Noon* was written before the WWII. Krymov's interrogator did not have names, just captain and investigator. *He was beaten up carefully, intelligently, by two young men in new uniforms who had an understanding of anatomy and physiology* p. 786).

Investigator Gletkin in Koestler's novel achieved his goal by receiving cooperation with Rubashov that makes the "Rubashov complex" only a part of the "Krymov comple"x. Besides the final fate of eventual extermination, Krymov's tragedy is deeper in the realization of the crush of his life beliefs and work.

The hide was being flayed off the still living body of the Revolution so that a new age could slip into it; as for the red, bloody meat, the steaming innards – they were being thrown onto the scrapheap. The new age needed only the hide of the Revolution – and this was being flayed off people who were still alive. Those who then slipped into it spoke the language of the Revolution and mimicked its gestures, but their brains, lungs, livers, and eyes were utterly different. (pp. 841-842).

Revolutions devour their children. This adage found its confirmation not at the time of the Great French Revolution when Robespierre of Danton was gone, but just less than a hundred years ago. The "Krymov complex" is one of its embodiments.

Krymov Abarchuk's introductory puzzle

There are puzzling factual mistakes when Krimov talks about Abarchuk (Ludmila Shaposhikova's first husband) : *"Once, in* **Petersburg**, *he was leading a platoon attacking the Winter Palace. He was full of fire and passion. I saw him a second time in the Urals.* **Kolchak's** *men had stood him in front of a firing squad, but somehow he got away with his life".(.Stalingrad. Page 151.}*

At Grossman's time, everyone in the Soviet Union knew that the stormed Winter Palace was renamed in 1916 Petrograd and Kolchak fought in Sibiria, not the Urals. while the Urals were mostly Czechoslovakia troops area. Grossman and editors could catch easily this mistake. Maybe, just the editors insisted on them for unknown reasons.

As a person who lived in Leningrad from the 1950s till the return of the Petersburg name, Leningrad was not referred to as Petersburg, Piter (Питер) was in common use.

I believe that Grossman intentionally put these words in the mouth of the Communist Party lecturer Krymov in the Stalingrad novel. Robert Chandler, main Grossman's translator, and Yurii Bit-Unan (Grossman scholar) disagree.

In my view, Krymov is presented by Grossman in *Life and Fate* with more sympathy than in the *Stalingrad* novel. The last sentences about Krymov in the *Life and Fate* novel when Krymov received in prison a parcel: *Krymov read through the list of contents: onion, garlic, sugar, white rusks The handwriting was familiar. At the end of the list was written: 'Your Zhenya'. 'Oh God, oh God.' He began to cry.* (p. 847).

Katsenelenbogen

During the intermission between beating interrogation, Krymov listened to his cellmate Katsenelenbogen, the old chekist who was part of the interrogative division of KGB but was arrested during the periodical changes of the staff purges. Smart and educated, he represented the clinical part of the Krymov Complex outcome in the extreme when the purge becomes a virtue. *Katsenelenbogen was a poet, the laureate of the State Security organs(.page.848)*

As a part of every life, Katsenelenbogen told Krymov *"how, in 1937, they had executed people sentenced without right of correspondence every night. The chimneys of the Moscow crematoria had sent up clouds of smoke into the night, and the members of the Communist youth organization enlisted to help with the executions and subsequent disposal of the bodies had gone mad."*(page 849).

Katsenelenbogen's cynical rhetoric which he poured into Krymov in general rigid mind of a Bolshevic looks like a step in the formation of the "Krymov complex", the tragedy of a believer who lost his faith. In contrast to Krymov, Katsenelenbogen was completely aware of when and how he crashed. He built a theory of a universal GULAG system, unpractical though dangerous, that provided him with mental stability after realizing the consequences of his work as a chekist.

However, in my view, the entire Katsenelenbogen pages in the Life and Fate novel were placed by Grossman to discuss the GULAG system issue when it is brought to the extreme.

Life inside the camps could be seen as an exaggerated, magnified reflection of life outside. Far from being contradictory, these two realities were symmetrical. Katsenelenbogen spoke not like a poet, not like a philosopher, but like a prophet. (page 845).

Grossman needed these pages of GULAG in 1960. Aleksandr Solzhenitsyn's *One Day in the Life of Ivan Denisovich* was published in 1962 and *The Gulag Archipelago* appeared abroad in 1970.

In Katsenelenbogen's project even Solzhenitsyn's In First Circle principle of a "charashka" is present. Nataly Frenkel's contribution to the development of the Gulag system is described. The imprisoned 'Nepman' became a lieutenant-general in the MGB – the boss appreciated the importance of his ideas. (page 844).

In Solzhenitsyn's The "Demon of the Archipelago", Frenkel is, first of all, a Jew in *The Gulag Archipelago. It looks like Grossman anticipating Solzhenitsyn's seminal book with Jews as main villains in Gulag's management, intentionally used an explicit Jewish last name for Katsenelenbogen.*

Abarchuk Magar

As the "Krymov complex" phenomenon, Abarchuk cannot be separated from his teacher Magar when they had met in the Gulag camp. Abarchuk presents the rigid Marxist revolutionary orthodoxy that is incapable of reaching the "Krymov complex" final regret *(His faith was unshakeable, his devotion to the Party infinite.* (p. 179). Just as "The party cannot be wrong," Rubashov said in *Darkness at Noon.*

His teacher Magar let him sit on the bed where a dead couple hours ago peasant, *kulak*, was lying. Some excerpts from Magar's talk: *First. We made a mistake. And this is what our mistake has led to. Look! You and I must ask this peasant to pardon us . . . No repentance can expiate what we've done. Secondly. We didn't understand freedom. We crushed it. Even Marx didn't value it – it's the base, the meaning, the foundation that underlies all foundations. Without freedom there can be no proletarian revolution . . . Thirdly our faith is stronger than anything. But this faith of ours is a weakness – a means of self-preservation. On the other side of the barbed wire, self-preservation tells people to change – unless they want to die or be sent to a camp. And so Communists have created idols, put on uniforms and epaulets, begun preaching nationalism and attacking the working class.* (p. 193).

Abarchuk responded in the end: *'I'll come and see you again. I'll put you right. I'll be your teacher now.'* But 'He [Magar} *hanged himself during the night.'*

'Suddenly Abarchuk sat up. He thought he had seen a shadow close by in the darkness.' The last sentences about Abarchuk in the novel. A shadow is his killer. (p. 194).

Mostovskoy

Mostovskoy, an old-time Bolshevik, represented the rigid Marxism line, incapable of change. Despite some doubts, he followed the communist orthodoxy. He could not accept the Ikonnikov's kindness manifesto, but he was upset when German fascist Liss called him a teacher *'Do you understand me, teacher?... 'Teacher,' he* [Liss] *said, 'you will continue to teach us and continue to learn from us. We shall think together.'* (page 403.)

Unfortunately, by presenting the" Krymov complex", Shimon Markish did not formulate the signs of it as a social and personal phenomenon. As a reader of Grossman's duology, I would suggest an approximate, far from psychology science, manifestation of the parts of it, that are displayed in the novel's main characters: doubts, frustration, and regret.

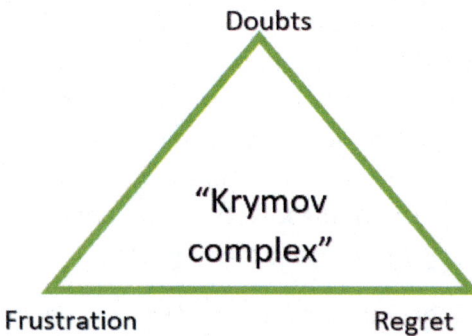

Doubts

"Krymov complex"

Frustration   **Regret**

Grossman's "Krymov complex" requires serious psychological and sociological study. The current notes are the introduction for such a study with the hope that a professional will undertake this task. I'm unable to do this work.

Koestler's novel was published in 1940 when the Second World War already started. Its publication in 1945 allegedly influenced the election by tipping the balance against the Communists in France in 1946.

Remarkably, in his review for the *New Statesman* in 1941, George Orwell praised Koestler's *"Darkness at Noon"*. Orwell underlined that Rubashov's tragedy was in his inability to answer the question: For what am I fighting? This was the title of Orwell's review.

Darkness at Noon is still in permanent circulation in libraries. The book is discussed on the Internet. Although it is not now a set text in schools, people continue to read this seminal book in thinking about fundamental human problems

Unfortunately, Grossman lived in the Soviet Union's informational bunker. He certainly was not even aware of the *Darkness at Noon* novel, as well as of George Orwell, Hannah Arendt, and other his contemporaries in the West. Both Jews, Arthur Koestler and Vasily Grossman, came through their experiences to the same conclusion of fascism and communism sameness in seminal fiction prose books of the 20th century.

Darkness at Noon can be found on Barnes & Noble bookstore shelves. Koestler's thin book should stand together with Grossman's the *Life and Fate* almost 900 pages novel. Although voluminous books are not currently in favor, Grossman's should be an exception. The new generation should learn from Krymov's mistakes.

A Writer at War book

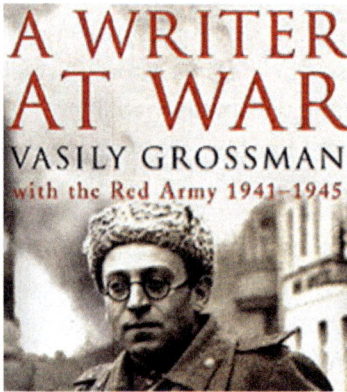

 A civil person in a military coat with a detached shoulder strap, more likely a Jew, looks at you among German city ruins from the cover of the book. This is the Red Army correspondent Lieutenant Colonel Grossman. The devastating war helped him to open or clarify for himself many sides of life, personal, national, and social. He placed his observations in notes and some letters. After the war, he tried to present them in his literary work. In 1964, he died never seeing them in print. On the other side of this page, circled publication requisites data of the book underline that the notes came to the public more than forty years after Grossman had died. However, better than never.

The copyright holders, his daughter, Ekaterina Vasilievna Korotkova-Grossman and Elena Fyodorovna Kozhichkina, the granddaughter of Grossman's stepson Fyodor Borisovich Guber, who owned Grossman's home archive, collected and edited Grossman's military Notebooks (Dnevniki). The notes are incomplete, electively selected, and censored. Some materials were obtained from the government's archives. This book was originated through translation into English and editing by Antony Bevor (historian, author of Stalingrad novel study, among other books) and Luba Vinogradova (translator, writer, biologist by training). The book was published in many countries. Remarkable that the book does not have a Russian edition. It cannot appear in the current ideological environment in the Russian Federation.

The front-line notebooks, which in many ways served as part of working material for the Stalingrad and Life and Fate duology, are now of interest to the reader in the West where Life and Fate is considered one of the literary masterpieces of the XX-century. Even some literary descriptions are disseminated in the notes which later could be found in the novels, like the terrible dust of retreat or the breath of war reaching the burned city.

The special value of the notebooks is their sincerity and critical view of the events described. We can follow the growing anger in his soul against the incompetence of so many commanders in their readiness to throw the lives of regular people without remorse into the furnace of war. On the other hand, the notes reflect the willingness of people to sacrifice themselves for victory.

Accused by some in the Russian emigrant press of
Russophobia after the *Everything Flows...* publication,
Grossman was impressed by Russians' heroism during the
war. For example, such lines: "In war, the Russian man wears
a white shirt. He may live in sin, but he dies as a saint." Or
"We Russians do not know how-to live-in holiness; we can
only die as saints. The front is the sanctity of Russian death,
and the rear is the sinfulness of Russian life".

It is remarkable that in his letter to his wife or father, we do
not have any critical remarks because every letter from the
army undergoes military censorship, Grossman complained
to his wife about editors in the *Red Star* newspapers. For
example:

The editorial office has adopted a rule of cutting off the end
of any essay, replacing dots with commas, crossing out the
descriptions that I particularly like, changing titles, and
inserting phrases like: 'This faith and love virtually made
miracles.' This editing is done in haste by professional
editors, and sometimes I have to read a phrase several times
to understand its meaning. All this upsets me very much
because I am working in very difficult conditions . . . (p. 198).

He could not for many reasons place in his reports and even mention as some winks such a passage about the private meeting with the commander of the 62nd army defended Stalingrad:

Great people produce a heavy, bad impression. Not a single word about the fallen men, about memorials, about immortalizing the memory of those who never came back. Everyone is only talking about themselves and their accomplishments. Morning with Gurtyev. The same picture. There's no modesty. 'I did it, I, I, I, I, I . . .' They speak about other commanders without any respect, recounting some ridiculous gossip: 'I was told that Rodimtsev said the following . . .' The main idea is, in fact: 'All the credit belongs to us, the 62nd Army. And in the 62nd Army, there's just me. All the others are unimportant.' Vanity of vanities.

According to David Ortenberg, editor-in-chief of the Red Star newspaper: Grossman remained true to himself. In Stalingrad, Vasily Semyonovich used to spend days and nights with the main characters of his articles, in the in the heat of battle."

Grossman could only trust a notebook of uncensored remarks. The private notes are often more interesting than the printed work because they are not self-censured. He knew that editors and authorities would never allow him to write about the extermination of Jews in Ukraine.

His article about the events in Berdichev *'The Killing of Jews in Berdichev'* was censored reducing emphasis on Jews so that Jews did not look like the main victims of the Nazis and camouflaging the degree of voluntary collaboration assistants by Ukrainians in the atrocities. the Stalinist position on Soviet suffering – 'Do Not Divide the Dead' – and partly because the involvement of Ukrainians in the anti-Semitic persecution was embarrassing for the authorities. The subject of collaboration during the Great Patriotic War was almost entirely suppressed. Grossman would soon find out for himself when he continued to investigate the operation of the Holocaust in Central Europe, the Poles, despite their anti-communism, were quite unlike the Ukrainians. Very few had collaborated with the Nazis.

The notebooks reflect Grossman's humanism and empathy. There are lines about mass rapes, looting, robberies, murders of civilians, and aimless destruction of property by soviet soldiers in Germany.

An educated German whose wife has received 'new visitors' – Red Army soldiers – is explaining with expressive gestures and broken Russian words, that she has already been raped by ten men today. The lady is present. "Terrible things happen to German women," he writes. Even "Soviet girls released from the camps are suffering today."

Women's screams are heard from open windows. A Jewish officer, whose whole family was killed by Germans, is billeted in the apartment of a Gestapo man who has escaped. The women and girls [left behind] are safe while he is there.

When he leaves, they all cry and plead with him to stay.
Grossman emphasizes the Jewish officer. (p. 327).

Quotes from A Writer at War book's Afterword:

Some of Grossman's Red Star articles were reprinted in a
small volume called Gody Voiny (The Years of War). The book
was circulated in several foreign translations.

 Grossman worked long hours on his novel about the
disasters of 1941, which he decided to call The People
Immortal, drawing heavily on his notes taken at the front.
The book became a huge success among the soldiers of the
Red Army. Grossman, a Jewish intellectual from another
world, had not just proved his courage at the front, but
above all the accuracy and human sympathy of his
observation.

 In general, the book authors' comments in the Afterword
aren't valuable, in my view. They are sometimes
understandably superficial and present well-known or
confusing data (the Story of Life and Fate manuscript
preservation). The statement that Grossman suffered from
stomach cancer is just wrong.

Grossman's sharpness of his observation and the humanity of
his approach to life around him provide invaluable lessons for
any reader. Grossman's notes in the book A Writer at War
are a significant addition to understanding his evolution
during the war. He went from an unconditional Soviet patriot
to a sober observer who fueled his postwar time books by
filling them with deep philosophical content.

If You Believe the Pythagoreans play's appeal

Before the war with Germany, Grossman wrote a play If You Believe the Pythagoreans. Remarkable, that the play was scheduled for reading in the prominent Moskow Vakhtangov Theatre on June 23, 1941, but the war with Germany began on June 22, one day before. The play was published in 1946 and heavily criticized by the Communist Party Agitation Department (Agitprop). As Russian scholar Yury Bit-Unan demonstrated in a special study, the criticism "has been occasioned by the rivalry between the Soviet Writers' Union and so-called "Agitprop". However, this rivalry was only on the surface. The main reason for conscious or intuitive objection to the play was the "If you Believe" in the play's title. In the country, where the History of the All-Union Communist Party (Bolsheviks): Short Course book, edited by Josef Stalin himself, was at the level of unchallengeable Bible, any philosophical "IFs" were very undesirable. Just at that time, the Communist Party's crackdown on the ideology front had started.

The play was not Grossman's best literary work and it is justifiably forgotten. Neither in Russia nor abroad this play is of interest even to scholars. This play is now interesting because of WHY and WHEN it was written rather than about What the actors would interact on the stage. However, it reflected Grossman's search for interpretation of changes in people's views of the world. He could not discuss openly under the conditions of the authoritarian country.

For him, as an intellectual, could not be unnoticed the fast change in people's views when Germany's perception was changed in a couple of years from the fascist country, which was fought during the Spanish civil war, into a friendly regime. The word fascism disappeared from the official propaganda language and most importantly also among the general population.

Grossman took from the Pythagoreans philosophy only the notion of a cyclic form of events. For Grossman might be important in this play, which was written in strong traditions of soviet literature, is the appeal to think about basic issues in life. For sure, Grossman was aware that the general population didn't know the Pythagorean philosophy existence. The targeted audience was the intellectual elite, the minority remained in the country after numerous purges. Even this minority stopped to ask questions becoming just followers as the rest of the country.

I would define the play as a proclamation leaflet placed on a visible spot for common attention. He wrote specifically a play, not a story or pamphlet, although Grossman was not a dramatist by his writing style. In Russian cultural tradition, theater performances also formed the society's attitude to social life. Great Russian actors emphasized the stage issues that the spectators were ready to hear. This was a time before TV. Movies were for the general population, but theater was for the elite. In a totalitarian country, the general population has zero influence on the government's power. Josef Stalin often attended theatrical performances.

Why, however, did Grossman publish the play immediately after the war in Znamya magazine in 1946? There is a notion that the play was written as a way of earning money. Of course, a professional writer is interested in royalties. However, it is too simple an explanation. Grossman was at the top of his writing career. He could and did republish his previous books and military correspondences. The play, in my view, was presented to the public just during the writing of *Stalingrad* with, perhaps, *Life and Fate* in mind as a sequel. At that time, this was Grossman's appeal to rethink the results of war, the price of victory. Stalingrad battle was a military victory, but the soviet people's defeat. This was one of the Stalingrad novel's points. The authorities wanted from Grossman a war epopee like War and Peace, but Grossman had in mind a philosophical drama because during the war all people's qualities became on display. Not by accident, just in 1946, Grossman suggested to wright a study on F.M. Dostoevsky that was not accepted by the publishers. Dostoevsky was not in favor of the soviet authorities at that time.

Forgotten as a leaflet proclamation on a pavement, the play is mentioned now only in the list of reference sources or about the critical reviews in some newspapers at the time of publication. I'm using a disproportionally large space in the current notes about the play because, in my view, Grossman started his transformation before the war with If You Believe Pythagoreans play, continued with Stalingrad (For a Just Cause) during the war, and finished with Life and Fate after the war. He was changing to the end of his life in 1964.

Journey to Armenia and An Armenian Sketchbook

Some introductory words

Vasily Grossman had a certain affinity for poetry, although no evidence of his poetry literature is called poetry. I assume he restrained himself, but in *An Armenian Sketchbook*, the last main book, he included many quotations from poetry. While in *Stalingrad's* novel, we do not see any, there are many quotations of poetry in *Life and Fate*. Poetry quotations are disseminated in letters to his friend Semyon Lipkin, a poetry translator and poet himself. Fyodor Gruber, his stepson, remembered that Grossman often read him poetry.

Grossman was formed as a person and a writer at a time when the revolutionary explosion stimulated poetic experimentation, staying on the shoulders of the Silver Age of poetry in the twentieth century. which began when its main representatives were still alive in Russia or had emigrated.

Mandelstam perhaps was the closest to Grossman among the poets in Russia in the twentieth century, especially during his end life. Like Grossman was and counted himself as a Russian prose writer, Mandelstam treated himself as a Russian poet.

There is a funny story about Mandelstam's strange behavior in a publishing house when irritated by the unfair long wait in a secretary lobby of a publication office he shouted: "I'm a Russian poet!" and left the room slamming the door.

In the 1930s, religious affiliation and national identification did not have such distinctions as it has today. For Grossman who was formed in secular times, it has no sense at all. But for Mandelstam, the distinction had cultural and esthetic meanings. Mandelstam assumed poetry as a product of gradual development from Greek through Judaism, toward Christianity's Western wing. The Russian intellectual Jewish "branch", which belonged, for example, to Boris Pasternak the main or Alexander Galich less, leaned to Orthodox liturgic Christianity. For completely secular Grossman, Mandelstam was closer.

As a product of the development of the October Revolution, Grossman embraced the internationalistic militant mood of poetry. The main bearers of this kind of poetry were ethnically Jews, but it did not matter at that time. Mikhael Svetlov (Sheikman) wrote a poetic bestseller *Grenada* (1926) about a Ukrainian peasant who fight in Spain to help peasants get farming land. The prominent poet Eduard Bagritsky (Dzubin) wrote a poem The Lay of Opanas (1926) where the main characters, Opanas and a Jewish commissar Yosif Kogan, interacted in complicated tragic relationships. Fyodor Guber wrote that Grossman had read him this poem aloud.

However culturally, Grossman was far from the revolutionary Jewish poets, like Eduard Bagritsky who wanted to depart from his Jewish heritage. The latter, in his brilliantly crafted poem "Origins", had lines: *"Above my cradle, rusty Jews crossed the blades of their slanted beards...And all the hysterics of my fathers..."*

Grossman was on the same cultural level as Mandelstam by escaping the yeshiva education, with similar bookshelf collections, though on a different scale of struggle with Jewish ancestry and national self-identification. While Mandelstam worked on his Jewish identification with attractions and rejections, with emotional declarations eventually coming to the notion of Hebraic Jew, for Grossman his Jewish ancestry was simply a fact of life.

Perhaps, this extended introduction might be useful to the subject of the comparison of Mandelstam's *Journey to Armenia* and Grossman's *An Armenian Sketchbook*. Both Russian literature masterpieces add to each other by underling the contrasts determined by time, the style of the authors, and the goals. While Mandelstam emphasized the esthetical and biological part of life, Grossman's attention was concentrated on philosophical and national issues.

Tribute to Osip Mandelstam

Osip Mandelstam's *Journey to Armenia* has its separate value as an event of literature. But it is chosen for these materials solely for a display of connection with Grossman's *An Armenian Sketchbook*. While Life and Fate intentionally follow Tolstoy's *War and Peace* structure, it seems that there is apparent *An Armenian Sketchbook* allusion to Mandelstam's Journey to Armenia. Undauntedly, Grossman was familiar with Journey to Armenia which was published in Leningrad's "thick" magazine *Zvezda* in 1933.

Grossman followed Mandelstam's *Journey to Armenia's* structure by interchanging details of the travel for readers' attention, insertion basic premises, and semi-fictional characters. Mandelstam includes in *Journey to Armenia* a multitude of scattered wonderful completely fresh poetic associations. Grossman as a hidden poet, is less generous in *An Armenian Sketchbook* in this regard, but cannot resist indeed.

An Armenian Sketchbook is a tribute to Mandelstam. His name is mentioned in *An Armenian Sketchbook* many times: *Mandelstam's poems are splendid. They are the very essence of poetry: the music of words. Perhaps even a little too much* so. pp. 36-37 *or But there is an enchanting music in Mandelstam's poems, and some are among the finest poems written in Russian since the death of Blok...* (p. 37)

About Mandelstam in An Armenian Sketchbook: *Nevertheless, some of his poems, some of his lines, stand up against anything written since the deaths of Pushkin and Lermontov. And although Mandelstam was unable to shoulder the entire great burden of the Russian poetic tradition, he is still a genuine and wonderful poet. There is an abyss between him and those who only pretend to write poetry.* (p. 37).

Grossman was surprised that writers, whom he conversed with, didn't know Mandelstam's name. *And my acquaintances in Yerevan did not remember Mandelstam's visit to Armenia.* (p. 37).

Cradles of civilization

Differently exhibited, the assumption of Armenia as one of the cradles of Western Ideo-Christion civilization connects both Joseph's (Yosef Emilyevich Mandelstam and Yosif Solomonovich Grossman). Both poems in prose tell the readers that two people, Jews and Armenians, created this cradle on the sand of Palestine and stones Aragatz, at the foot of the biblical Mount Ararat.

In *Journey to Armenia*

For Mandelstam, who calls Armenia' 'that younger sister of the land of Judea", he walks in Yerevan with "Jewish staff", "elder's walking stick." Mount Ararat was 'rich with a Biblical carpet' in an Armenia cycle poem, Mandelstam is called a "Sabbath land." Grossman was certainly familiar with both Mandelstam's highest prose and poetry creations, as well as the Forth Prose. By the way, the latter was written in 1929, but has not been published but went around in the intellectual circles until 1966, in the United States, when both already died though in different ways).

In Grossman's Armenian landscape can be heard Mandelstam's "the stones and clay of Armenia, the whole primitive coloring of the thirsty land, place it in the Old Testament."

For Mandelstam, according to his widow Nadezda Mandelstam, the travel to Armenia was his journey to a place where first people adopted Christianity, "to this ancient civilization", "he went back to his origin."

As sounds in *An Armenian Sketchbook*

In An Armenian Sketchbook: "I knew some sweet and touching details about Mandelstam's time in Armenia and I had read his Armenian cycle of poems. I remembered his words about "an Armenian Christianity of beasts and fables." (p. 36).

Humanity's most important mountain—the mountain of faith —called up innumerable associations in my mind.

The Bible and the present day came together with astonishing ease, and I saw Mount Ararat through the eyes of people who lived on these mountain slopes before the birth of Christ. (p. 93).

I see Mount Ararat—it stands high in the blue sky. With its gentle, tender contours, it seems to grow not out of the earth but out of the sky, as if it has condensed from its white clouds and its deep blue. It is this snowy mountain, this bluish-white sunlit mountain that shone in the eyes of those who wrote the Bible. (p. 32).

The biblical myth of Mount Ararat seemed entirely contemporary. (p. 99); ...the stars that shone above Mount Ararat before the Bible even existed, (p. 99); Mandelstam was fascinated by Armenians' " ...noble inclination for hard work", and their surroundings by utensils a baking dish, a pair of tongs, and an earthenware jug with milk". Grossman's admiration for the same things is disseminated in An Armenian Sketchbook. He liked to watch the process of baking bread or see the wander of made-in-stone churches, as Mandelstam did.

Mandelstam's intellectual resistance

Mandelstam, with a poet's intuition, fought on the intellectual field at the beginning of the totalitarian regime, namely in literature, starting in the Fourth Prose in 1929. For Grossman, Mandelstam was an example of intellectual resistance. Against the well-wisher's advice not to publish, Mandelstam refused, and he could see it published. Grossman was not successful in seeing *An Armenian Sketchbook*. It was published after his death.

Journey to Armenia pages about biology are more as a tribute to intellectual freedom. Mandelstam could not know that his rather esthetical play with Lamarck would bring Trofim Lysenko a crash on genetics as a totalitarian regime's weapon of suppression. Grossman knew the result as a former full-blown socialistic realism representative in Soviet Union literature, where he was an active participant to his chagrin, and he asked for forgiveness in *An Armenian Sketchbook*. Grossman knew that after a short period of genetics resurrection during the "Khrushchev's Thaw", directly Khrushchev brought back Lysenko and all the devastation of genetics studies again.

Mentioning Mandelstam in *An Armenian Sketchbook* was a sign of Grossman's courage in his status of the outcast and the desire that An Armenian Sketchbook would be published. All water was gradually frozen after the "Khrushchev thaw" at that time just before Khrushchev's fall down.

When *An Armenian Sketchbook* was written, in 1962- 63, Mandelstam was not the intellectual circles household name, as it is now. Moreover, he, the greatest Russian poet of the 20th century, was not known at all. From an official document, issued to Osip Mandelstam's brother: "Rehabilitated posthumously on the 1938-year case (died in 1938 place of burial unknown — in the 1956 year, on the 1934-year case [Exile in Cherdin after the famous Stalin epigram]— in 1937 year." For about 20 years after Mandelstam's death, his very name was under arrest. Only in 1989, the publishing house "Khorurdain Grokh" published Journey to Armenia. It became Osip Mandelstam's second book published in the USSR during the Glasnost era.

Grossman was a poet who wrote only prose by hesitating to write pure poetry. Mandelstam wrote both. Poetry when he could write from voice. Mandelstam insisted that the method of prose differs from poetry stating that "Prose form is synthesis." Grossman tended to write synthesis. More than likely, Grossman was familiar with Mandelstam's Fourth Prose written in 1929. It was not published until 1966 (in New York, in 1988 in the USSR), but went around in intellectual circles.

Mandelstam's "advantage" was in emotional instability, to define this softly, with the attempt of suicide. Grossman was a down-to-earth completely stable and rational personality with many family responsibilities. This brings additional points to his courage. Often Viktor thought of two lines of Mandelstam: ... "The wolfhound century leaps at my shoulders, /But I am no wolf by blood." But this time was his own time...(*Life and Fate* p. 267).

Some personal remarks

 One personal detail might illustrate the social environment around Mandelstam's name at the end of" Khrushchev thaw" in the Soviet Union. In 1962 when An Armenian Sketchbook had been written, as a sign of trust, my college teacher made me familiar with the Mandelstam's famous Stalin epigram with a warning of not to disclose it to somebody. He wrote it on a piece of hard paper which I kept for a long time. I learned by heart this epigram with now immortal lines: Our lives no longer feel ground under them. /At ten paces you can't hear our words. Unfortunately, they do not sound in English so powerful. And now unfortunately again became so actual in Russia.

Again personal. *Journey to Armenia* requires me more education and intellectual capacity. *Journey to Armenia* looks to me like a sketchbook for the Mandelstam's Armenian poems cycle. The more you read these poems, you discover *Journey to Armenia's* facets in spontaneous lights reflecting from the carefully grounded diamond. The cycle was inspired by *Journey to Armenia* after five years of silence in writing poetry. *An Armenian Sketchbook* is incomparably closer to me than *Journey to Armenia* for many reasons, but the main of them is that I am Grossman's contemporary divided by some time, experience, and intellect. Grossman speaks to me, while Mandelstam talks about his Jewish identity.

Albert Camus and Vasily Grossman

Immediately after the Second World War, the French philosopher Jean-Paul Sartre published *Existentialism Is a Humanism* (French: L'existentialisme est un humanisme) book in 1946. Existentialism became the mainstream trend of philosophy among the intellectual elite in the West at the time of Albert Camus's *The Rebel (L'Homme révolté)* book publication in 1951.

There were fierce discussions and disagreements between leading philosophers at that time. For example, the famous German philosopher Martin Heidegger rejected Jean-Paul Sartre's book. Albert Camus also objected to Sartre's book, although he is remembered as one of the most important existentialist philosophers of the 20th century.

While having only superficial knowledge of philosophical theory, I believe that existentialism flourished not by accident among frustrated intellectuals after the devasting war with the loss of millions. The elite reflected people's desire for stability and tranquility in life. But the same was the attitude of ordinary people. I lived among survivors after the Holocaust as a teenager.

This short biography about Grossman is not the place to analyze Camus' seminal book of political philosophy, especially at my level of education. There is plenty of literature about it. I want only to extract some considerations that, on one hand, might help to support Grossman's place in Soviet Union literature of the second half of the 20th century as a reluctant rebel, and on the other hand, show that he was objectively, maybe unknowingly, in the line of European cultural development at that time.

Albert Camus' question in *The Rebel* essay

 I want to present Grossman's characterization as a reluctant rebel by appealing to Camus's famous quote:

'What is a rebel? A man who says no: but whose refusal does not imply a renunciation.' (emphasizes in bold and red added)

This phrase is part of the paragraph that follows the second sentence, which says: "He is also a man who says yes as soon as he begins to think for himself."

Camus published this question and an attempt to answer it in his *The Rebel* almost 300-page book-length essay. Camus to a high degree summarized his prewar thoughts about human nature and the course of the progress in social and cultural life.

The rebel's "NO" signifies a refusal to accept the predetermined fates and the constraints imposed by society, tradition, or external conditions. In other words, it represents an act of defiance against repressive forces or oppressive systems seeking to confine and define people's existence but does not simply renounce their current circumstances.

In his book essay, Camus shows that the 'No" means when the "slave who has taken orders all his life, suddenly decides that he cannot obey some new command." This led to rebellions with revolts which is one of the 'essential dimensions' of mankind, a principle of existence. But it is no longer the revolt of the slave against the master, not even the revolt of the poor against the rich; it is the revolt of man against the conditions of life, against creation itself. At the same time, it is an aspiration towards order through revolutions, predominately intellectual.

 Camus showed how inevitably the course of revolution leads to authoritarian dictatorship from Rousseau to Jacobins, Marx, Lenin, and Stalin with fascist counterrevolution in between. All revolutions in modern times have led to the enforcement of the power of the State. "The strange and terrifying growth of the modem State can be considered as the logical conclusion of inordinate technical and philosophical ambitions, foreign to the true spirit of rebellion, but which nevertheless gave birth to the revolutionary spirit of our time."

At the time of *The Rebel's* book publication, existentialism was a dominant philosophic-political trend among intellectuals in the West. Per Camus, being in a world filled with uncertainty, without a clear meaning of purpose, individual rebels challenge the status quo and refuse to conform, while still maintaining their fundamental principles and beliefs. Existentialism places rebellion as the main tenet of personal freedom, challenging the structures that want to restrict it. However, there are limitations to the rebel's "no" and this was Camus' point. The way to create a future goes through human efforts in the present.

Existentialism, as a philosophical and social tendency, had a predecessor in F. M. Dostoevsky's Russian classical literature of the 19th century. This partially explains the enormous popularity of Dostoevsky in the second half of the 20th century.

Remarkably, among a broad gallery of rebels in European civilization, rebels of Russian origin, resolutioners, and terrorists, Dmitry Pisarev, Mikhail Bakunin, Sergei Nechaev, Ivan Kalyaev, Vladimir Lenin, and others are discussed in Camus' essay. Characters of Fyodor Dostoevsky's novel "Demons": nihilists and terrorists (Liputin, Virginsky, Lyamshin, Shigalev, and others), as well as their inspirers and leaders (Nikolai Stavrogin and Pyotr Verkhovensky), are of interest for Camus. There is even The Path of Shigalev chapter in the essay. Dostoevsky's Ivan Karamazov is discussed as a rebel who cannot find his way to solve his problems. The same was Camus himself.

Camus had chosen to search for the defense and triumph of the universal values. Humanity is indefinitely greater than a single human being. An individual, having become a rebel defends the whole of humanity.

 By paraphrasing Descartes's "I am thinking, therefore I exist", Camus's formula was" I rebel, therefore we exist". The key word is "we", which means "collective action". Here is the crossroad where Camus and Grossman had met each other in the ruins of intellectual fields of Europe after the horrors of the ended war. They went in the same direction on the parallel roads.

Grossman's answer to Camus's question.

Perhaps Grossman was interested in philosophical issues. He wrote a play, *If You Believe the Pythagorean*, which was harshly criticized by the official press on ideological philosophical grounds, having never seen the stage. More important to our subject is that he suggested writing a book about F.M. Dostoevsky in 1946

At that time, Dostoevsky was not in favor of the Communist Party's ideological policy. Grossman's suggestion was rejected, perhaps for good, because of this fried time to write the duology, his life achievement.

At the end of the Second World War, Camus was already a world-renowned writer and philosopher. He was awarded the Nobel Prize in Literature in 1957 for writing the *Miph of Sisyphus* novel before the war. *The Rebel* was already published, while Grossman's *Stalingrad* novel underwent censors and self-censorship snags.

 Although Grossman knew French, it is doubtful that he was aware of Camus, especially under the conditions of an already full-blown Cold War. Of course, he could not have read *The Rebel*. He could not have known Camus's¬ question, but he answered in his way—boldly and constructively—in line with the European humanistic tradition of world civilization.

Grossman's humanism is part of the existentialism concept where individual freedom is the central tenet. Reluctant to take on a philosopher cloth, he presents the lamentation of freedom as a writer.

 In Stalingrad's destroyed 6/8 house (an allusion to Pavlov House during the Stalingrad Battle} before his inevitable death, captain Grekov said to Commissar Krymov.: "For freedom, I'm fighting". Ikonnikov, the Tolstovian philosopher, goes to death in a concentration camp defending his choice of refusal to participate in the building of a crematorium for murdered people.

Grossman was a living soul's admirer with an extraordinary ability to talk with a commander in an army headquarters, a soldier in a trench, a German prisoner, or even a dog and a cat. His war duology Stalingrad and Life and Fate are about people during the war. The last pages of Life and Fate are about two unnamed people known only to the reader. The couple goes on the road to get bread by stepping on melting spring snow. *Everything Flows...* ends with the main character, Ivan Grigorieviv, a former prisoner of Gulag, coming to see his home where his mother had lived with the vow to stand fast on his core beliefs. *An Armenian Sketchbook* so-called travelogue ended with a wedding description in a rural Armenian village where people maintained their traditions and shed tears of joy and sorrow.

Much nuance is lost without a general understanding of the novels, a reading of Grossman's books is crucial in fully grasping the interwoven narratives of this section. I hope that the insights derived from the short excerpts of Grossman's novels presented in this book will serve as an additional impotence to further explore his work.

Both Vasily Grossman and Albert Camus left Earth in the early 1960s without having known each other. It would have been fruitful communication between a writer philosopher and a philosopher writer.

Two failed Soviet authorities' projects

The second half of the twentieth century in the Soviet Union can be marked by two literature projects by Vasily Grossman and, in my view, Aleksander Solzhenitsyn. While Grossman's conscious or subconscious involvement in the project is almost undisputable, Solzhenitsyn's participation is more as an assumption, nevertheless, I believe, worth discussing.

Vasily Grossman as Red Tolstoy

After the Stalingrad battle victory, the Soviet Writer's Union establishment started to contemplate a gift to the Supreme Commander Joseph Stalin in the shape of the Soviet Leo Tolstoy-like *War and Peace* epopee. Vasily Grossman was the apparent candidate to carry out this project. He took on the unannounced open task with some enthusiasm in 1943.

With interruptions for his duties as a war correspondent, Grossman finished the first part of the book with the title *Stalingrad* in 1950. The novel's voluminous size, composition, language, and even some characters resemble Tolstoy's novel, perhaps sometimes intentionally. The tortious, on one torn even dangerous, ordeal of the publication is described in the *Stalingrad (For a Just Cause) novel* section of the current book.

However, the political and ideological environment had changed. Stalin had different priorities after the war. Grossman was not his favorite writer. The increase in governmental antisemitism was apparent.

There was a struggle between different branches of the ideological apparatus of the Communist Party that generated difficulties for the publication of this book. Eventually, the book was published in 1952 and generated a bone-breaking criticism at the beginning of 1953 during the "Doctor's Plot" time.

However, the *Life and Fate* squeal of the duology was so disappointing for Soviet authorities, that the KGB arrested the manuscript in 1961. Both novel's ordeals are described in many publications, including in the current book.

Below is the short chronology of the Soviet Red Tolstoy *War and Peace* epopee project.

1943-1949 Grossman wrote *Stalingrad (For a Just Cause)*.
1950-1952 Published in *Novy Mir* magazine after revisions.
1953 Harsh criticism during the antisemitic campaign, but eventually the magazine accepted the book for publication after Stalin's death.

1953-1959 Soviet authorities supported Grossman's work on the duology sequel by publication of his previous books.

1960 *Life and Fate* manuscript delivered to *Znamya* magazine.
1960-1961 Editorial assessment, consultation with Communist Party Ideological department.

1961,14 February, the KGB arrested the manuscript.

1962 Grossman's in vain efforts to get the manuscript back:

    February appeal to Polykarpov, the CPSU Agitprop head;

    February 26, the letter to Khruschev;

    July 23, meeting with Mikhail Suslov.

The end of the project.

Grossman kept the detailed chronology of the ordeal. It is interesting regarding the parallel development of Solzhenitsyn's *One Day in the Life of Ivan Denisovich* story scenario in the *Novy Mir* magazine and at the Communist Party headquarters.

Communist Party ideological front bosses' noble intentions provided them with a hot potato on their hands. They thought that they buried in the ground the unwanted potato for years. And they were right. *Life and Fate* was published in the USSR only in 1989, two years before the USSR disappeared from the world's map.

Aleksandr Solzhenitsyn as "Grossman -Lite"

Solzhenitsyn's case is more complicated. It includes some assumptions. Depending on the ideological point of view, political affiliation, and access to documents, there could be different approaches. Without being drowned in the pound of numerous conflicting literature data, I want to present my vision of Solzhenitsyn's *The Gulag Archipelago* phenomenon, as a project of different levels of Soviet authorities. It is supported by available open press-related materials. On one hand, my view is determined by my understanding of the social and political environment at that time in which I was a contemporary. On the other hand, it is based on my assessment of Solzhenitsyn's personality after reading his political statements and his autobiographical publications.

Assumption of Solzhenitsyn's project development

Two introduction remarks

According to Vadim Bakhtin, who headed the KGB in the last months of 1991 after the August 1991 coup, all the materials of Solzhenitsyn's "operational development" in the KGB, which amounted to 105 volumes, were destroyed in 1989-1990 by burning in special furnaces designed to eliminate documents. The burned folders contained tapes of eavesdropping and their partially printed transcripts, copies of letters, video recordings, denunciations of secret informants, etc. As archivists used to say: without a document, there is no argument.

Why? Almost thirty years after the events connected to
Solzhenitsyn were in actual spotlight. This could be a part of
the standard KGB operation for secret intelligence sources
and methods, but Solzhenitsyn could not carry any
governmental secrets unless some of them were undesirable
for authorities' connections. It was time for the end of
Gorbachev's "perestroika". The KGB understood the
direction of the political winds. It would not be reasonable to
elaborate with unsubstantiated guesses and accept the result
that many details will remain unknown unless they appear by
accident, but it is doubtful. By the way, the materials of
Grossman's KGB monitoring after the *Life and Fate*
manuscript's arrest were not destroyed.

The Solzhenitsyn case was purely political at that time. Some
words about the political atmosphere in the Communist
Party and in its pretorian guard branch KGB otherwise it
would not be understandable. The balance of power was
always swindling regarding how the party was dominating.

The periods related to the subject of the current sketch
consist of two main periods: 1962-1964, when Nikita
Khruschev was in power, and 1965 after Khruschev's fall.

Being the intrinsic part of Stalin's people's extermination
system, Khrushchev continued the ideological fight against
the so-called "Personality" cult", the euphemism of Stalin. He
also wanted to get rid of remnants of Beria in the KGB. Beria,
who inherited the concentration camps system was the
embodiment of it because he transformed it into an
industrial enterprise that could solve many projects,
including nuclear weapon development.

Khruschev hated Stalin for humiliation when the latter treated Khruschev as a court jester. Khrushchev's v was afraid of Beria. The apparatus was changing slowly after Khruschev had been dismissed. Vladimir Semichastny, a mediocre former Komsomol chief, remained as head of the KGB till 1967 when he was replaced by Yuri Andropov.

The Communist Party and KGB finally realized that Solzhenitsyn was a serious problem for them. The Nobel Prize in literature for in general unread stories and books, probably arranged through the same channels as Michael Sholokhov's prize, worked against them.

They wanted to have him outside the USSR. He did not respond to hints, including ricin poisoning in 1991.

In my assumption, the Solzhenitsyn project had two stages:

first, the *One Day of Life of Ivan Denisovich's* story, and second *The Gulag Archipelago* investigation.

In the first, the authorities used Solzhenitsyn, in the second, which was a continuation of the first, Solzhenitsyn used the authorities. When the latter realized this, it was too late for them.The genie of The Gulag Archipelago was out of the bottle, to the Soviet authorities' chagrin, which determined their rage against him. The Grossman-lite project turned out to be a self-inflicted wound by the KGB that could not be cured by Solzhenitsyn, the Nobel Laureate's imprisonment. Solzhenitsyn understood their hopeless position. He further irritated the wound with provocative writing like the Letter to the Soviet Leaders.

One Day in the Life of Ivan Denisovich story

Chronology

In May 1959, when Solzhenitsyn was living in Ryazan, he wrote Щ-854 (Sch-854), *One Day of One Zek Story*.

Khruschev made again an anti-Stalin speech at the Communist Party congress in October 1961. Solzhenitsyn sent the manuscript to the Moscow journal Novy Mir in November 1961 through his friend Lev Kopelev, who was his inmate in a prison camp for intellectuals with special research tasks (later called "sharashka".

The editor of the journal's prose section, Anna Berzer, passed it on to Novy Mir's editor-in-chief, Aleksandr Tvardovsky, who was eager to publish the story. After 11 months of editorial work with the manuscript, it was delivered to Khruschev with the help of one of Khruschev s deputies. The story *One Day in the Life of Ivan Denisovich* [romanization Odin den iz zhizni Ivana Denisovicha] was approved by Khrushchev. On October 12, 1962, he pushed through the decision to publish it at a meeting of the Presidium of the Central Committee of the CPSU (Politburo).

The story appeared in the November 1962 issue of the magazine under the title *One Day in the Life of Ivan Denisovich*.

November 17 - 18 – 1962 the issue of the Novy Mir with "One Day" goes to subscribers and appears on sale (immediately sold out).

December 17 -1962 Solzhenitsyn participates in a meeting of state leaders with literary and art figures at the Reception House. Solzhenitsyn was accepted into the Soviet Writers' Union on 30 December 1962. (One story writer was accepted into the Union!).

March 7-8 - Solzhenitsyn at a meeting of state leaders with literary and art figures in the Catherine Hall of the Kremlin.

In December 1963, One Day in the Life of Ivan Denisovich was nominated for the Lenin Prize by the editorial board of the Novy Mir magazine and the Central State Archive of Literature and Art.

According to the *Pravda* newspaper (February 19, 1964), he was selected "for further discussion." The Lenin Prize was not awarded (April 22, 1964).

Comments and Assumption

The Soviet Writers' Union was under the direction of the Communist Party Central Committee. The surveillance of the KGB was not tight at that time. There was an apparent propaganda campaign with the implementation of the Communist Party line of the condemnation of the previous penitentiary system connected to Josef Stalin and Lavrenty Beria, the system's face, times.

Irrelevant to the rest of the country, but significant for the Moskow intellectual elite, the shock after Grossman's *Life and Fate* novel's arrest was still lingering. Grossman was still active in his efforts to get back the manuscript. He wrote a letter to Nikita Khrushchev and met with the head of the ideology department Michael Suslov. His department apparatchiks had read the novel where such powerful pages were devoted to the prison system that later was named GULAG, actually the abbreviation, which became a noun in the world's vocabulary.

An obscure writer from Ryazan, the author of two printed stories was suddenly invited to meetings of the Soviet intellectual establishment This can be explained only as a Communist Party propaganda department was in charge of a project through its intellectual branch, the Soviet Writer's Union, and the KGB, security supervision, sometimes action, as in Grossman's case just two years ago had occurred by Life and Fate manuscript arrest.

The Communist Party ideological department needed a writer who could continue the assault on the prison system, read Lavrenty Beria's stronghold, project. Ivan Denisovich was a gift for the project. Solzhenitsyn could be such a writer. They wanted something like "Grossman light".

The Gulag Archipelago

Chronology

According to Solzhenitsyn's second wife Natalya Dmitrievna Solzhenitsyn (Svetlova), The Gulag Archipelago " was written by Solzhenitsyn in the USSR secretly in the period from 1958 to 1968 (completed on February 22, 1967??). The in bold "according" is because she was not his wife at that time (Natalya Alekseevna Reshetovskya was) and the timeline is important.

This time should include a shortened variant of In First Circle («Circle-87») in 1964 and Cancer Ward novels presented to Novy Mir magazine in 1966. Both novels were not published in the USSR until 1990.

Comments and assumptions

Nomination for the Lenin Prize inevitably brings a person to the KGB "operational surveillance". The secret department of the Lenin Prize Committee receives from the KGB a "dossier" on all candidates. While preparing the materials, KGB staff noticed that Solzhenitsyn was during his imprisonment an informer with a secret title Vetrov.

Khrushchev was still in power in 1963. He was ousted by the Communist Party leadership on October 14, 1964.

The KGB chief Vladimir Semichastny was aware of Khruschev's attitude toward "Beria's" concentration camps. Solzhenitsyn was the best candidate to explore this subject because Ivan Denisovich was still a story without a greater picture.

While living in Ryazan and working as a teacher in a school (left only in 1964), Solzhenitsyn could not just physically produce so many voluminous books without real help.   The most important is that material in The Gulag Archipelago included secret data (camps, staff, history, etc.) which he could not get from any source, except from KGB or another official course twenty years before "glasnost" time arrived during Gorbachev's "perestroika".

Even physical dwellings in a provincial city required effort at that time. Everything was a problem, including getting food and wood for a stove. Of course, incomparably better than life conditions immediately after the war. It was not enough to have a camera to make copies. The development t of the film was time-consuming and required conditions and reagents, which were not easily available outside big cities.

I assume that during Khruschev's time in power, Solzhenitsyn received help from different government sources, especially the KGB. Although the inertia of cooperation might continue after Khruschev's demise, the KGB became suspicious of Solzhenitsyn's efforts to hide his material. We cannot know if the KGB was aware of the photo film that was sent abroad even in the fall of 1964, but Solzhenitsyn's archive was taken from friends Teush and Zilberberg in September 1965.

The rest of the events would not add substantially to confirm or object to my assumption that The Gulag Archipelago was a soviet authority and Solzhenitsyn mutual project during Khruschev's time in power. Solzhenitsyn deceived his KGB partners. Or they want to be deceived for some reason.

Again, in summary, *The Gulag Archipelago* project, which was carried out under the Communist Party Ideological branch auspices with the help and monitoring of the KGB, failed. Solzhenitsyn was better than the KGB, a movement ahead in this chess game. He played some gambits on his terms.

KGB's rage against Solzhenitsyn was determined by frustration that he deceived them with *The Gulag Archipelago*. Solzhenitsyn exploded his victory by becoming the dissident number one in the Soviet Union and the world.

Headed by Nikolay Kryuchkov (one of the initiators of the August 1991 coup), the KGB was interested in incineration materials related to Solzhenitsyn that could conceal their blunder and other circumstances related to Solzhenitsyn. Perhaps, the truth will be never known.

At this point, I want to stop to elaborate on my assumption which I cannot prove. Two different personalities in life and with different fate outcomes. Two projects failed by intent, but were great by outcome. Grossman created *Life and Fate*; Solzhenitsyn produced *The Gulag Archipelago*. Both were the indictment of the Soviet regime. Grossman's mine was defused by authorities.

Grossman outfoxed the KGB by hiding the *Life and Fate* manuscript among two trusted friends. This reflects also how deeply he knew the system.

Solzhenitsyn learned from Grossman's debacle. He outfoxed the Soviet authorities. As a result, objectively it was the KGB's blunder that allowed to place one of the mines under the Soviet totalitarian system.

Grossman and Solzhenitsyn

Two writer's bombs under Soviet ideology

Vasily Grossman and Alexander Solzhenitsyn are two Soviet writers of the second half of the 20th century still relevant in the current century as political philosophers. It is difficult to imagine two more different persons by views, temperament, and fate of life.

Aleksander Solzhenitsyn is a well-established name in the West. Vasily Grossman's name is completely unknown. He is more known by literature scholars in the West. In the Russian Federation, he is almost completely forgotten by the general public, as well as ignored by scholars with some exceptions, for example, David Feldman and Yuri Bit-Unan.

This article is an effort to change the wrong assumption of these writers not only for historical fairness but also for the necessity to draw attention to their differences in moral and political issues, which are highly important and relevant in the current time when modern civilization is adjusting to new challenges.

Robert Chandler, Grossman's English translator, said in a 2022 interview: "...often people I don't know write to me out of the blue and say almost in identical words, "Reading *Life and Fate* changed my life." I suspect that part of the reason for this is Grossman's emphasis on moral choice. There are a lot of moments in his work when people are faced with moral choices of life-and-death importance."

Alexander Solzhenitsyn, the writer, who introduced to the world vocabulary the word GULAG, deserves world recognition and respect. The word "gulag" has come to mean any sort of labor camp for political prisoners. But "gulag" isn't a word—it's an acronym for Glavnoye Upravleniye Ispravitelno-Trudovykh Lagerey, which means "Chief Administration of Corrective Labor Camps" in Russian. Moreover, it was designed not only for political prisoners. It was a sophisticated system of a mixture of political and regular criminals with the dominants of the latter.

The word "zek" (zakluchenny, "convict", prisoner) appears in the Russian language at the suggestion of Solzhenitsyn. The destruction of Soviet ideology begins also with the *One Day of Life of Ivan Denisovich* story. And, of course, *The Gulag Archipelago* was an exploding bomb.

In the 1970s, we read *The Gulag Archipelago* on translucid typed paper clandestinely in a forest 30 miles from Leningrad, in the Soviet Union. Later, *The Gulag Archipelago* copy on a thin paper was kept as a treasure. It is shared only with trusted friends. Just in case, the book was kept out of home.

Personal relationships

Grossman had never met Solzhenitsyn. When Grossman died in 1964, his name was well known. He was in the first cohort of soviet literature writers in prose. He was even a member of the Soviet Writers' Union board. Solzhenitsyn was a rising fine literature star in the Soviet Union and abroad after *Novy Mir* magazine published in 1962 and 1963 three stories, including *One Day in the Life Ivan Denisovich*. The *Life and Fate* novel, which was delivered to *Znamya* magazine in October 1960, was arrested on 14 February 1961.

Grossman's ordeal with *Life and Fate* inevitably circulated among the relatively closed group of the writer's community where *Novy Mir magazine* was the epicenter. Anna Berser, the *One Day in the Life Ivan Denisovich* "midwife", could arrange this meeting being one of the closest Grossman's friends.

Grossman undoubtedly would be interested to meet the writer of the story, which he had read with enthusiasm. He continued to work with *Everything Flows...* to the end of his days. In general, he cut relationships with the writers' community, especially the establishment, which, in his view, betrayed him. Solzhenitsyn would be an exception.

Avoiding any contact with a rebel writer, Solzhenitsyn was technically right. The open KGB archives showed that Grossman was under close surveillance. Even his home conversations were documented. There could be other Solzhenitsyn considerations that we cannot know and should not guess.

Grossman as Solzhenitsyn's predecessor

Solzhenitsyn is commonly perceived as the sole person who opened the world's eyes to the Soviet vast network of prison camps. It is correct only to some degree. Before *The Gulag Archipelago* with a somehow puzzling subtitle *An Experiment in Literary Investigation* was published in 1974, the Soviet penitentiary system was explored by few publications and in some memories. However, the essence of the system was displayed by Vasily Grossman in his *Life and Fate* novel finished in 1960. A few chapters in the voluminous *Life and Fate* (Rubin's murder in the camp and Krymov's interrogation in the Lubyanka prison) would be the best illustration of *The Gulag Archipelago*'s three volumes. The same can be said about the insert novella in *Everything Flows...*about "quiet Mashenka" Lyubimova who has traveled the entire martyr's path of the camp during a year.

Shimon Markish, the scholar, who was mentioned many times in the Appendices of the current book, wrote: *"Everything flows...* anticipates *The Gulag Archipelago*. Some of the camp chapters are quite consistent with the genre definition that Solzhenitsyn gave to his work as an experience of artistic research. ... Of course, there are differences between the embryo and an adult, but the same plan, the same goal, the same - in potency – strength of generalizations and accusations."

The GULAG was discussed in a conversation between Krymov and Katselenbogen in the Lubyanka prison cell. (page 844). All main points of the Solzhenitsyn's *The Gulag Archipelago* are in these conversations.

As Markish remarked about the *"quiet Mashenka" story: "It was written in the spirit and key of the quiet lamentation, the strangled howl of a mourner... Grossman's special voice is irreplaceable and necessary in the polyphony of the camp requiem" Grossman preceded "A Woman in a Camp" chapter in Volume Three of The Gulag Archipelago with a memorable emotional lamentation."*

Solzhenitsyn's statistics, data, and stories are impressive, but Anna Grigorievna's story on a couple of pages in *Everything Flows...* provides a breathtaking picture of the extermination of Russian and Ukrainian peasantry by the regime. These pages were written well before *The Gulag Archipelago*. They will stay. I'm unsure about *The Gulag Archipelago*. I remember Mashenka's story since we distributed samizdat *Everything Flows...* copies in the 70th.Solzhenitsyn could also obtain a copy when he wrote *The Gulag Archipelago* and after, being abroad. He never mentioned it. Solzhenitsyn was shy to call Grossman his predecessor.

In this regard, it is remarkable to read his *The Oak and the Calf*, a 500-page memoir, written in 1967 with supplements in 1971, 1973, and 1974. This book is interesting by itself as a textbook of self-promotion and a display of Solzhenitsyn's personality. *Everything Flows...* was already published at that time in the West, but the novelette was not mentioned, although Solzhenitsyn knew it.

Solzhenitsyn already started to build the fence against Grossman, his main competitor on the Russian literature second half of 20th century pedestal.
The last punches he did 30 years later in 1999 and 2003, especially in *Vasily Grossman's duology* article published in *Novy Mir* magazine. This article will be discussed later.

Grossman's name appeared in *The Oak and the Calf* memoir five times. It is worth presenting them in their entirety. Out of context, they are unclear, but it does not make sense to go into detail. Nevertheless, direct quotes are remarkable, although look boring and superfluous.

First (page 27), in a Novy Mir editorial squabble in parentheses (This happened with V. Grossman's stories, for instance). Second, (page 101. "I remembered how Grossman's novel had been taken from that very safe at Novy Mir. "Third. (page137) Allegedly Tvardovsky said*: "It's like Grossman writing about the camps from hearsay.* "Fourth (page 302). In a footnote about Suslov's talk with Grossman about the confiscated novel and Ivan Denisovich's story was a surprise to authorities.

Fifth (page 460). In Appendixes a remarkable sentence: "More than that, they have been exposed to violence and personal persecution (Bulgakov, Akhmatova, Tsvetayeva, Pasternak, Zoshchenko, Andrey Platonov, Aleksandr Grin, Grossman). This is the end of Grossman's presence in the memoir.

The level of accuracy of this list is disputable, by the way. Only Grossman's manuscript was arrested. No any on the list *"have been exposed to violence and personal persecution."*

Differences and similarities in basic concepts

Now, when these priority issues belong to history and should be tied to the conditions of that time, more important to concentrate on the interpretation of Grossman's and Solzhenitsyn's concepts. Perhaps would be interesting to discuss Grossman's differences with Solzhenitsyn on more basic conceptual grounds. Moreover, it would be useful to see them in the frame of Solzhenitsyn's other publications.

In this regard, the analysis of difference had been presented by Shimon Markish in his *Grossman's Example* book published in 1985. Shimon Markish was a supporter and admirer of Solzhenitsyn's fight with the official Soviet regime just to 2003, when Solzhenitsyn published his *Two Hundred Years Together* book and *Vasily Grossman's Duology* article in *Novy Mir* magazine. The book about Grossman is only in Russian. Now it is a rarity. This is the reason that I placed extended quotes from this book.

Here are some excerpts from this book:

"Solzhenitsyn narrowed his point of view on Stalin's crimes, strictly limited time and place (which cannot be attributed to his achievements). Grossman, in Life and Fate, committed the cardinal sin of generalizing "individual cases" and thus attacked the very ideological basis of the regime.

He spoke about the same thing in a different way, with a different historical philosophical, and most importantly - human position.

His intransigence and intolerance to the lies and evils of communism are not inferior to Solzhenitsyn's, but the scale and measure of values are different. He does not believe in the nation, but in the individual, he calls not for collective repentance and not for self-restraint, but for individual "senseless kindness" - unselfish, unreasonable, inexplicable. And he yearns not for God, not for religion, not for destroyed age-old traditions, but for freedom, which Russia has never known in a thousand years of its existence. "

Markish underlined that the central in Grossman's position is the conversation with Mostovskoy in the prison camp, actually Liss's monologue, which ended with a crucial phrase: *"Teacher, you will always teach us and always learn from us."*

As Markish wrote, *"Solzhenitsyn always stopped to equalize the communist and Nazism regimes and ideology. In 1960, to draw such a parallel openly, in print meant condemning oneself to death, if not physical, then at least literary: after all, none of the Soviet writers had yet dared to do anything even remotely similar."*

Markish remarked that in *Life and Fate* the theses of Solzhenitsyn's famous article-appeal "Live not by lies!", written more than a decade and a half later; *"... the most important of Viktor Shtrum's line, the future Solzhenitsyn motif sounds - the motive of repentance. While different in the main concept, Grossman preceded Solzhenitsyn as a writer also on the basic moral issues."*

Solzhenitsyn's Jewish problem

The "Jewish" part of *The Gulag Archipelago* looks now differently in the light of following Solzhenitsyn's literary work. There were many alarming places of animosity toward Jews there, for example, the second volume of *The Gulag Archipelago* with its abundance of Jewish names and photographs in the story about the founders and builders of the system of "extermination-labor camps". Solzhenitsyn explained later that only these photos were in his possession at that time.

Solzhenitsyn concentrates on one of the founders of the GULAG system specifically as a Jew: "Naftali Aronovich Frenkel, a Turkish Jew", with the following phrase: "It seems to me that he hated this country." Repeated later on August 14th "thirst for revenge on Russia."

Solzhenitsyn offered to Russian Jews in "August the Fourteenth": Let everyone decide for themselves and firmly adhere to his decision - either to say to Russia "I am yours, and you are mine" or "to join in the patient process of history".

Much later, in 2002, in *Two Hundred Years Together*, a two-volume book about the history of Russian Jewry, Solzhenitsyn claimed that Jews shared the blame and responsibility for the Revolution and other Russian problems of the twentieth century, as well as for troubles before.

Already many times referred to Shimon Markish in his 2003 Solzhenisyn Judeophobe article noticed that these premises could be seen already in The Gulag Archipelago. A Jew, Parvus, was responsible for the October 1917 Revolution. An ugly Jew in the camp raped a girl who was described as a bucolic Russian beauty. And so on.

Especially dear to the Russian "patriots" was suggested by Solzhenitsyn the prospect of repentance of Jews before the Russian people, which they, convinced to alcohol consumption. Of all these topics, he seriously discusses only one which forms the nerve of his entire book: the mutual guilt of Russians and Jews in the 20th century.

Perhaps, the main gilt is that Jews were most in the group that were facilitators of the Russian nuclear weapon project, as well as other weaponry industry areas. Now Russia threatens the world.

As Shimon Markish wrote: "That is why Judeophobia is - psychosis, illness, inadequacy. And Solzhenitsyn, for all his "troubles" on the Jewish theme, is still quite adequate. He is just "a little pregnant" with anti-Semitism."

Solzhenitsyn's *Vasily Grossman's Duology* article

Solzhenitsyn published *Vasily Grossman's Duology* article in *Novy Mir* magazine in 2003. Besides nitpicking some factual discrepancies in the novels, he did a condescending, almost humoristic some places review of Grossman's approaches.

Solzhenitsyn already discussed Grossman's work in a patronizing way in the *Novy Mir* publication in 1999. As Yuri Bit-Unan, a Russian scholar on Grossman, jokingly wrote: *"The legislator of the new Russian prose* [Solzhenitsyn] *regularly appeared in the Novy Mir magazine as a critic. He also paid attention to the author of Life and Fate: he was awarded a slightly above average rating."* The same tone remained in Solzhenitsyn's 2003 publication.

 Solzhenitsyn was correct in underlining that many places in the *Stalingrad* novel sounded just from Soviet propaganda rhetoric lines. For example, the Soviet Union was defined as*" a great nation that had already the foundations of a future world."* The commissar Krymov leads his soldiers holding his Communist party membership card. *"Rarely in his life had the essence of Soviet unity seemed so clear to him. ... Nazis hoped to undermine this unity"*. And so on about the unity of Soviet people in Soviet Russia. Grossman, who was on the front lines and could also communicate with high-ranking military and Party bosses, had more broad experience during the war than Solzhenitsyn, the captain in an artillery sound protection battery located far from the battles. At the beginning of the war, when the regular army was destroyed, commissars often led some military troops (Grossman's *The People Immortal* and Krymov in *Stalingrad* novels).

Grossman needed to publish this book at any cost of compromises with editors and censors. After *The Black Book* debacle, he needed to use *Stalingrad*, the first book of the duology, as a Trojan horse to insert the Jewish line. Viktor Shtrum appeared quietly in the 27 chapters through his wife Ludmila Nikolaevna and is more than a side story about her first husband Abarchyk. In the article, the latter is inequitably a Jew for Solzhenitsyn which is right, but Grossman intentionally hid this circumstance.

Specifically, Solzhenitsyn concentrated on the Jewish line in the *Life and Fate* novel. A mixture of humor and gall. There could be presented numerous examples. This was not the right tone in such a sensitive area.

As a writer, Solzhenitsyn performed worth and worth with every new production from the first published *One Day in the Life of Ivan Denisovich*. Would be better, if Solzhenitsyn had not written this article that crippled and devalued Solzhenitsyn's literary production and even legacy. Perhaps, Solzhenitsyn felt this. Self-dissatisfaction fuels often antisemitism even in well-accomplished people. Never mind felt nation and countries.

Shimon Markish wrote in 2003: "*Solzhenitsyn the rebel left his imperious imprint on everything that came out in print, whether in samizdat under his name. The spell dissipated only with the second version of "August the Fourteens'...Neither "Two Hundred Years Together" nor other similar opuses, which, perhaps, will still come out from the pen of Solzhenitsyn, will change it. ... Everything he prints is weak, bland, tasteless. He had written himself out.* "

Different concepts of Mother Russia

Mother Russia is a common definition in Russia. The sculpture "The Motherland Calls!", part of the monument ensemble "Heroes of the Battle of Stalingrad ", was erected in Volgograd in 1967. There is a line from Grossman's Direction of the Main Thrust sketch written during the WWII Stalingrad battle in 1942.

Although Grossman and Solzhenitsyn had not come across each other, there was a traceable intellectual dispute between them concerning the vision of Mother Russia. It was not only due to their different ages, characters, and cultural backgrounds, the concept of nationalism was entirely different in their literary works.

Grossman's internationalism could not accept Aleksandr Solzhenitsyn's Russian Slavophil-type nationalism. Part of the Soviet Russian emigration unjustifiably accused Grossman of Russophobia in the unpublished *Everything Flows*...novelette. Solzhenitsyn had not objected to these unjustified accusations. But Grossman, unaware of these accusations because he died ten years before, had anticipated them. He tried to clarify his vision of Mother Russia in also unpublished *An Armenian Sketchbook* in the form of just remarks in this travelog.

During his "Jewish Journey" after the Second World War, Grossman remained his Mother's Russian son. He hadn't found any discrepancy in this dichotomy. In his literary work, Grossman assumed Russia as an intrinsic part of European Judeo-Christian culture.

Grossman and Solzhenitsyn's different concepts of Mother Russia can be simplified by two words: land or people. This difference was reflected in the characters of their literary work. While for Solzhenitsyn people were in the abstract form of a group's," village", spirituality, for Grossman people were just his surroundings.

Solzhenitsyn's second published story Matryona's House (or Place) [romanization Matryonin dvor], is considered to be one of his finest literary achievements. In the story, the entire village is populated by ugly grid people. Only Matryona was like a saint. Of course, we understand that these people lived under awful conditions in the Soviet Union.

There is an allusion in the choice of Matryona's name to a mother [мать] in Russian. The initial title of the story *was It Is Not Worth A Village Without A Saint*. The story ends with the following phrase: "She is the righteous saint, without whom, according to the proverb, there is no village or city. Not all our land." Matryona is a symbolic metaphor for suffering Mother Russia. Solzhenitsyn's nationalism represented the concept of Mother Russia as land, a large village. This story, along with all following literary work, reflects the grim truth that Solzhenitsyn loved his country as a Russian nationalist, but was not a fan of its people.

In contrast, Grossman liked both, but more people who have to dwell in this country. We can see Grossman's love in his books' characters.

Grossman wrote about cultural exchange between people in Russia. Grossman noticed with satisfaction the Russian classical stove in the kitchen of a peasant in an Armenian village. For Grossman, the value of Russian empire expansion was not in the territory but the opportunity to bring Russian culture which he treated as a development of the Western civilization.

The current Russian authorities' justification of the war in Ukraine can be found in Solzhenitsyn's letter to the recently elected President of the Russian Federative Republic B. N. Yeltsin on August 30, 1991, five months before the Soviet Union collapsed.

Excerpt from the letter: *"**Russia retains the right to revise its borders with some of the seceding republics. This is especially acute with the borders of Ukraine and Kazakhstan, which were arbitrarily carved by the Bolsheviks. The vast south of today's Ukrainian SSR (Novorossiya) and many places on the Left Bank [Dnipro River] have never belonged to historical Ukraine…**"*.

These views Solzhenitsyn expressed later, for example in an interview with the New Yorker's magazine David Remnick in 1994. Solzhenitsyn's fundamental ideas formed the basis of Vladimir Putin's policy. Moreover, Solzhenitsyn himself, at the end of his life supported Putin.

In 2000, Russian Prime Minister Vladimir Putin visited Solzhenitsyn for a consultation about the school program's curriculum. They more than likely discussed not only the school curriculum programs. Vladimir Putin had other conversations with him.

In 2003, Putin gave a speech during the gathering of Russia's military establishment in the Air Force Academy where he declared anti-West change of Russia's foreign policy. It resonated with Solzhenitsyn's views.

Putin visited Solzhenitsyn in 2007. The so-called Putin's Munish speech at the Munich Security Conference in February 2007 where thunders of future storms could already be heard. In 2008, Russia invaded Georgia.

Solzhenitsyn's views were repeated in speeches of Russian authorities and the propaganda before and after the invasion of Ukraine in 2014, and eventually on 24 February 2022.

Solzhenitsyn's seeds sprouted bloody poppies that intoxicated Russia. Solzhenitsyn placed bricks in the background of the ideological support for the devastating war in Ukraine, which will certainly damage or even eventually destroy Russia.

We can assume, with some certainty, what side of the battle Grossman and Solzhenitsyn would stand on; two Russian writers in the middle of the 20th century during Russia's unprovoked invasion of Ukraine at the beginning of the 21st century.

Solzhenitsyn and Grossman in modern Russia

Solzhenitsyn

Solzhenitsyn became a living classic of Russian literature. In the 30-volume collection of Solzhenitsyn's works, "The Red Wheel" occupies 10 volumes. Solzhenitsyn was one of the main moral authorities of the Russian official state at the end of the 20th century and remains today. The "how to live" prophet had also aroused criticism. A dissident Vladimir Voinovich wrote a satiric novel about him.

The abbreviated version of *The Gulag Archipelago* was included in the school curriculum, although there are now voices in the Russian parliament ("Duma") to exclude it because of changes in the official attitude toward the KGB; which was renamed FSB.

In December 2018, Putin unveiled a bronze monument to commemorate the 100th anniversary of the writer's birth on Solzhenitsyn Street in Moscow. Bronze monuments were erected in Russian cities Vladivostok and Kislovodsk (Solzhenitsyn's birthplace).

The Aleksandr Solzhenitsyn Center (Ignat Solzhenitsyn, President, Stephan Solzhenitsyn, Executive Director, sons) hosts the official English-language site for Aleksandr Solzhenitsyn.

Grossman

Grossman technically exists in Russia, but he is invisible. A few memorial plaques are scattered on insignificant buildings. In 2009, on International Holocaust Remembrance Day, a memorial plaque was installed on the wall of the house in which Grossman lived. (Kranoarmeyskya Street, 25).

The *Life and Fate* novel was staged by Lev Dodin in Sankt Peterburg in 2007. It is doubtful that it would be done now. The play was on the stage more abroad than in Russia. The TV four film serial on *Life and Fate* novel (2012) would not be possible now.

Even the 2014 documentary Vasily Grossman: "I Realized That I Died" (2014) by Elena Yakovich could not be produced now. The film shows the official transfer of KGB (now FSB) from the "Special Folder" of Vasily Grossman, the arrested Life and Fate manuscript to the Russian State Archive of Literature and Art.

On May 17, 2021, the Russian Federation president's spokesman was asked about the Life and Fate ban possibility because, according to the new law, equalization Nazism and Stalinism would be a crime. His answer was ambiguous. He did not object to the possibility.

As Grossman's translator Robert Chandler said in an interview in November, 2022:" Grossman would be liable to be in prison for things he wrote in it. Drawing a direct parallel between Nazi and Stalinist policies is a criminal offense today."

Epilogue

Grossman and Solzhenitsyn or Solzhenitsyn and Grossman. Two completely different personalities. Grossman can be an example of Solzhenitsyn's antipode. The prominent Russian writer, Grossman's friend, Andrey Platonov used to say: "You're the Christ, Vasya." His reputation as a person was impeccable during his life and remains today. His character was difficult because he had high moral standards for himself and expected decency from others.

At age 85, Solzhenitsyn wrote *Darkeners are Not Looking for a Light* sketch in his efforts to clear his name from wrong, in his view, accusations. To some degree, he was right, because the KGB relentlessly wanted to damage him very much, in my view, in retaliation for the blunder by allowing him to create *The Gulag Archipelago* under close secret service monitoring.

On the other side, it was impressive the number of people who wanted to help him, his friends, and well-doers, although the KGB involvement could not be excluded.

 In *The Oak and the Calf*, he describes in humiliating detail people who even helped him, for example, Aleksandr Tvardovsky. The described people are not angels, but the narrator looks ugly. The oak (the Soviet system) is rotten, but the calf (Solzhenitsyn) behaves like a hog digging under the roots in the famous Russian fable.

Grossman had not had to write an acquittal autobiographical opus. He could not write such a sketch soaked with gall. His last book was titled *Good for You! People*.

Both Vasily Grossman and Aleksandr Solzhenitsyn were rebels at their time. Grossman was a kind, humanistic rebel. I am unsure that the same adjectives could be applied to Solzhenitsyn. In my view, just the opposite would be right.

Grossman was a reluctant rebel while pointing out the similarity between totalitarian communist and Nazis regimes which destroys human beings. Solzhenitsyn's vindicative rebellion was in the Bolsheviks' accusation of the Russian Empire's destruction and the formation of the Gulag system with the help of Jews.

I am biased.

Solzhenitsyn's *The Gulag Archipelago* is a milestone in the Soviet penitentiary system accusation. However, he takes Grossman's place as a great Russian writer of the second half of the 20th century unjustifiably. Solzhenitsyn, perhaps, suspected that he was a mediocre writer. Grossman was on his way to becoming the last classic of Russian literature, but his writing talent and skills were not adequate for this task.

Solzhenitsyn remains in fine literature at the level of *An Experiment in Literary Investigation*, as he called *The Gulag Archipelago* in the subtitle, and his entry in fine literature story *One Day in the Life of Iwan Denisovich* despite his voluminous books' heritage.

Grossman was a great fine literature writer, as Solzhenitsyn wanted to be. Maybe, these notes might contribute to the dethroning of Solzhenitsyn from the pedestal of the great Russian writer, while leaving him at a well-deserved place in the history of shaking the communist totalitarian regime in the Soviet Union and around the world. This was his undisputable achievement.

Just as 19th-century Dostoevsky became in demand in the 20th century, the second half of 20th-century Grossman is relevant to the beginning of the 21st century. The fracture of the established world order manifested in the war in Ukraine, which can also be seen as a result of the abandonment of humanism principles that propagated Grossman's literary work. The world needs Grossman.

The Goddess of Justice Femida, despite keeping the bandage on her eyes, probably follows the current political, cultural, and fashion tracks with one or even both eyes open when issuing verdicts. Her scales are often rigged by a heist of superficial judgments. History Goddess Clio is not in a hurry. She will keep for future generations the communist and Nazis regimes' guilty verdict in Vasily Grossman's *literary work*. Aleksandr Solzhenitsyn's *The Gulag Archipelago* will be an important footnote document in the Soviet totalitarian regime's indictment of it.
I rely on her.

Printed in Great Britain
by Amazon